The Arc of the Covenant

The Arc of the Covenant

Jewish Educational Success on the Upper Mississippi

Earl Schwartz

LEXINGTON BOOKS
Lanham • Boulder • New York • London

Published by Lexington Books
An imprint of The Rowman & Littlefield Publishing Group, Inc.
4501 Forbes Boulevard, Suite 200, Lanham, Maryland 20706
www.rowman.com

6 Tinworth Street, London SE11 5AL, United Kingdom

British Library Cataloguing in Publication Information Available

Library of Congress Cataloging-in-Publication Data
Names: Schwartz, Earl, 1953- author.
Title: The Arc of the Covenant : Jewish educational success on the Upper Mississippi /
    Earl Schwartz.
Description: Lanham, MD : Lexington Books, [2019] | Includes bibliographical
    references and index.
Identifiers: LCCN 2019019766 (print) | LCCN 2019020981 (ebook) |
    ISBN 9781498596671 (electronic) | ISBN 9781498596664 (cloth : alk. paper)
Subjects: LCSH: Jewish religious education—Minnesota—Saint Paul—History—
    20th century. | Educational planning—Minnesota—Saint Paul—History—
    20th century. | Jewish religious education—Teaching methods.
Classification: LCC BM70 (ebook) | LCC BM70 .S266 2019 (print) |
    DDC 296.6/809776581--dc23
LC record available at https://lccn.loc.gov/2019019766

∞™ The paper used in this publication meets the minimum requirements of American
National Standard for Information Sciences—Permanence of Paper for Printed Library
Materials, ANSI/NISO Z39.48-1992.

Contents

List of Figures

Preface

It is my hope that the following chapters might prove useful, first of all, to the members of the Jewish community of St. Paul, Minnesota, as they grapple with the challenges of developing and implementing an educational plan for the community. To its credit, the Jewish Federation of St. Paul initiated a long-term Community Planning Process in 2012 that emphasizes the importance of educational planning for the whole community. *The Arc of the Covenant* is intended as a resource for this ongoing planning process.

However, to the extent that the challenges the St. Paul Jewish community is facing are not unique to St. Paul, I hope that what follows might prove helpful to other communities as well. For the past five years I have immersed myself in the institutions that are the subject of this book. I taught once again in the St. Paul Talmud Torah Midrasha and Day School, served on the Educational Panel of the St. Paul Federation's Community Planning Process, and spoke about the history and future of Jewish education in the Twin Cities at numerous gatherings in both St. Paul and Minneapolis. In each of these ways I sought to engage the current realities of Jewish education as fully and broadly as possible, while studying the story of Jewish education in St. Paul through archival research and interviews with many of its principal figures. I come away from these experiences convinced, more than ever, that a school isn't just one community institution among others, but the foundation upon which all other Jewish institutions ultimately depend, as the *halakhah* regarding the relative sanctity of schools and synagogues suggests. Jewish communities cannot pray or play their way to viable futures, but we may yet find our way, through learning.

Insights to be garnered from the pages that follow are from many sources. I have had the pleasure of speaking with dozens of community members and researchers about the issues I explore. My sincere thanks to all who shared their time and insights with me, including Harry Adler, Ken Agranoff, Carol Carlson, Susan Cobin, Arnold Dashefsky, Kate Dietrick, Marty Dworkin, Burt Garr, Ruth Gavish, Barry Glazer, Rabbi Joel Gordon, Loraine Hertz, Rachel Levitt, Dorothy Lipschultz, Sol Minsberg, Sara Lynn Newberger, Jonathan Paradise, Jon Parritz, Marvin Pertzik, Elyse Rabinowitz, Cindy Reich, David Rischall, Randi Ilyse Roth, Nina Samuels, Jeffrey Schein, Linda Mack Schloff, Harold Smith, and Dalia Vlodaver. And my sincere thanks as well to Mikayla Mislak at Lexington Books for her editorial assistance.

I am deeply grateful to all those who have helped me to better understand my subject. Any errors in the pages that follow are my own.

And a special word of appreciation to Anna Kleinman Schwartz, indomitable eighth grade American history teacher at Lincoln Junior High School in North Minneapolis, in the 1960s. In the course of my research, we met again for the first time, when she was a new arrival in St. Paul, one hundred years ago.

In the summer of 1976 I crossed the Mississippi from North Minneapolis to St. Paul's Highland Park to teach at the Talmud Torah of St. Paul. The community won my heart, and I've never left. It is with deepest appreciation for my years at the Talmud Torah of St. Paul—for all I've learned there—that I dedicate *Arc of the Covenant* to its students, teachers, administrators, staff, and friends.

ויהיו בעיניו כימים אחדים באהבתו אתה
Genesis 29:20

A synagogue may be turned into a school, but a school may not be turned into a synagogue, as the sanctity of a school is greater than the sanctity of a synagogue, and we may add sanctity, but we may not decrease it.

—Maimonides, *Mishneh Torah, Hilkhot T'filah*:11:14

Introduction

A persistent despair wends its way through Jewish history: unprecedented neglect of Jewish learning portends communal collapse. Even in the period of the Talmud, as the rabbinic movement was rising to ever greater prominence, prominent figures bemoaned *yeridat ha-dorot*—the decline of successive generations: "If those of former times were angelic, we are human, and if they were human, we are like asses."[1] Maimonides repeatedly expressed despair over the condition of Jewish learning in his day. In the introduction to his *Mishneh Torah* he mourned, "In these times, stricken by severe troubles that threaten all, 'The wisdom of the wise among us has disappeared, the understanding of the prudent among us is hidden.'"[2] In the sixteenth century, David Provenzalo, a prominent member of the Jewish community of Mantua, Italy, introduced a proposal to establish a Jewish university with the lament, "because of our manifold failings, the intelligent Jews are diminishing; how the learned are disappearing from among us without there being anyone able to take their place . . . and this generation, the children who are now being born and are growing up after the setting of our sun, act just like those who have never seen the light."[3] In his poem "l'Mee Ani Ameil?"/For Whom do I Labor? (1873), the Russian Jewish poet Yehudah Leib Gordon conveyed his despondency with particular irony. Dismayed by the rapid gains of assimilationist initiatives he himself had once vociferously championed, he now asked (in Hebrew): "Might I be the last writer of Hebrew poetry, and you, its last readers?" The labor Zionist leader Yaacov Hazan is credited with the assessment, "We wanted to raise a generation of non-believers, and we raised a generation of know-nothings."[4] And a 100 years after Yehudah Leib Gordon, Yehudah Amichai, still writing in Hebrew, would close his fitful meditation on hymn "Ein K'Eloheinu" with the bitter observation that though

1

perhaps something was finally stirring in an impassive God, "*aval ha-am ha-Yehudi k'var nigmar*—but by now the Jewish people is finished."[5] The last Jews, yet again. "But if we are the last," as Simon Rawidowicz would conclude in the generation that saw both the mass murder of the Jews of Europe and the establishment of the State of Israel, "let us be the last as our fathers and forefathers were the last. Let us prepare the ground for the last Jews who will come after us, and for the last Jews who will rise after them, and so on until the end of days."[6]

Such is the impossible task of Jewish education—building a bridge between "the last" and "the next." Here stands the contemporary Jewish educator, executor of a will and testament the heirs aren't eager to hear, a peddler of dissonance, fearful of failing both the past and the future, in a world where Jews constitute a shrinking "part of the main," cantilevered over the most unlikely places—St. Paul, Minnesota, for example.

To be sure, when the context is specific enough—the last Jews of a particular ideological orientation, or of a certain location—end points can be found. But even within such limits the record has not been so clear. Time and again Jewish communities, Torah in hand, have revived, evolved, or returned. The complexity of any one Jewish community, let alone all Jewish communities, helps to explain how this could happen. Sundry social and cultural strains crisscross Jewish history, forces of regeneration intercepting swaths of decline. Sometimes these forces are unforeseen, other times appearing too alien to be recognized as regenerative. But as Kierkegaard observed, the tale can only be told in retrospect, and from this perspective the story is not only of unremitting, inexorable decay, but also of dry bones that have lived again. That there aren't more Jews at the beginning of the twenty-first century, living in more inspired and inspiring communities, is sobering, but that there are any at all is astonishing. Rawidowicz went so far as to suggest that perhaps reiterating despair has been an effective coping mechanism for the onerous duties incumbent upon a people responsible for escorting history to its proper conclusion. Just as lucidity required that biblical prophets first flee their calling before hearing it, so too, Jewish communities, must flee so daunting a duty before they can engage it.

By the 1960s American Jews appeared to evidence yet another reason for pessimism. As the great majority set their sights on the socioeconomic mainstream, Jewish institutions and distinctive Jewish practices were in dramatic decline. And yet, research from the period suggested that Jewish education remained a potent counter-influence. St. Paul was the site of one such research project, perhaps the first in the United States to focus on the relationship between Jewish education and adult Jewish identity. The 1969 study of young Jewish men in St. Paul indicated that Jewish education was a significant predictor of adult Jewish identification—provided it extended into adolescence,[7] a conclusion substantially affirmed by Geoffrey Bock in his 1975 study *Does Jewish Education Matter?*[8] Harold Himmelfarb would add the stipulation that the effects of Jewish education became statistically significant only after 3,000 hours of schooling.[9] As the last quarter of the twentieth century began, these findings could be seen as hopeful. Education, after all, was a foundational feature of rabbinic culture, a familiar facet of all contemporary Jewish movements, and long touted, in St. Paul and elsewhere, as an elixir for renewed vitality. Effective Jewish education could be reason for hope—if not for the fact that teenage enrollments were low and contact hours were dropping.

As the century progressed and research continued, the ills identified in the accumulating reports on St. Paul and other communities across the country remained relatively consistent: too little cooperation among communal institutions, inadequate faculties, too few hours, conflicting messages at home; layer upon layer of discouragement. And then, something in St. Paul appeared to be going right—a little miracle on the Upper Mississippi. Arnold Dashefsky, coauthor of the 1969 study highlighting the continued significance of Jewish education in shaping adult Jewish identification, would maintain that particular features of the St. Paul community helped to account for these successes, features that were both the product of fortuitous circumstances and thoughtful planning.

The internal dynamics of the community Dashefsky studied, its place in the larger social fabric and its constituent institutions, appeared quite similar to those of numerous other American Jewish communities: a medium size city with a relatively small Jewish community and an aging river town on the Upper Mississippi. Given these characteristics, it would not have been surprising to learn that the St. Paul Jewish community, like many others, had been wilting for decades. Instead, in the latter decades of the twentieth century it underwent a period of remarkable vitality, stimulated, in large part, by a jolt of educational renewal and achievement. As this regenerative surge was cresting, Kim Marsh, executive director of the St. Paul United Jewish Fund and Council, would celebrate these developments as "harbingers of our future success."

As the profile of the St. Paul community rose in Jewish educational circles, attention would be focused primarily on what St. Paul Jewish educators were then doing, while the specific factors that had precipitated a flourishing educational environment in so unlikely a locale, aside from Dashefsky and coauthor Howard M. Shapiro's general observations, went largely unnoted. The primary intent of what follows is to more directly connect those contributing factors to the educational successes that ensued, with the hope that doing so might help to rekindle the educational energies of the St. Paul community, along with other communities facing similar difficulties.

To *rekindle* the St. Paul community's educational energies, as this isn't simply a story of achievements. By the beginning of the new century, prospects for Jewish education in St. Paul appeared once again to be arcing downward, and with it, Marsh's vision of "future success." This, too, is a story worth telling, though some might ask "Why?" Why care about one more community now also in decline—a mid-sized, Midwestern, largely middle-class Jewish enclave on the Upper Mississippi? Why even care *in* St. Paul, let alone "down river"?

There are two primary reasons for careful consideration of St. Paul's story. First, be they relegated to "up river" or "flyover" territory, the Jewish communities of the Midwest have, in fact, been home to an exceptionally large number of gifted Jewish educators, skilled communal workers, and progressive initiatives, far out of proportion to the size of their populations, as compared with larger Jewish population centers.[10] In his "The National-Cultural Movement in Hebrew Education in the Mississippi Valley," Daniel J. Elazar chronicled the exceptional vitality and educational effectiveness of the "Talmud Torah" form of communal educational agency in several Midwestern locales, including St. Paul, through much of the twentieth century:

> Not only was the Talmud Torah the major product of these educators, the Talmud Torah flourished and reached its maximum strength in the Mississippi Valley, especially in the smaller Jewish communities of the Midwest: Superior, Wisconsin; Indianapolis, Indiana; Omaha, Nebraska; Akron, Dayton, Columbus, Cincinnati and Cleveland, Ohio; Minneapolis and St. Paul, Minnesota; and Detroit, Michigan. This was true as late as the 1970s. Where the Talmud Torah survived in the postwar generation as more than a fossil remnant, it was in the same medium-sized and smaller Jewish communities of the Mississippi Valley in which it had flourished earlier.[11]

In this and other similar passages in Elazar's work, one finds the beginning of an answer to the question "Why care about what happened decades ago in St. Paul?" And yet, outside of Elazar's and Dashefsky's interest in the question—and despite widespread recognition that *something* of import had occurred in the Twin Cities—surprisingly little has been written about the relationship between local educational initiatives and the specific characteristics of the communities in which they occurred, including St. Paul. Moreover, Elazar's 1993 monograph doesn't cover more recent developments, references to the community are in some cases inaccurate or insufficiently detailed, and Elazar's specific interest was in the "national-cultural" Hebrew language and literature-based focus of the schools he highlighted.[12] Given the promise of the developments he describes, the seeming unlikelihood of their emergence in St. Paul, neglect of the topic by most other researchers, and an absence of more recent reflection on the specific factors identified by

Dashefsky, Shapiro, and Elazar as leading to these developments, a closer look at St. Paul's place in this regional story is warranted.

But in addition to the historical value of a closer look at the history of Jewish education in St. Paul, there is a second, more practical, value as well. Many Jewish communities demographically similar to St. Paul are approaching social and cultural twilight: not yet moribund, but largely devoid of impetus. In reflecting on the story of Jewish education in St. Paul, we are confronted by the challenges such communities face, and the decisive role communal education can play in meeting such challenges, not as theoretical or statistical abstractions, but as lived experience. Communities of a significantly different size will likely embody different social dynamics, but similar-sized locales could well benefit from its example—that is, communities that may be near to larger urban centers with bigger Jewish populations, but are still large and diverse enough to benefit from consideration of how a similar populace has dealt with educational opportunities and discord.

There's nothing mysterious or unique about the people in this story, but as Dashefsky and Shapiro suggested, there is something "illuminating" about the confluence of factors, decisions, and relationships that shaped Jewish education in St. Paul in the twentieth century that make the story well worth telling. The establishment and growth of the Talmud Torah of St. Paul, representative of American Jewish hopes invested in the Jewish "community school" model as it took shape in the early to mid-twentieth century, stands at the center of this story. An accurate rendering of these developments requires careful consideration of the Talmud Torah's origins and subsequent role in the community.

In as much as this is a study not simply of schools or community, but of schools *in* a community, the range of sources consulted and interviews conducted have extended well beyond historical, demographic, sociological, and educational research and experts alone. Active community members, some now well into their nineties, communal agency directors, and founders and alumni of St. Paul Jewish schools were also consulted, along with archived interviews of numerous twentieth-century community members. What follows, then, isn't a tour of educational theories and artifacts, but an attempt to tell the story of a particular Jewish community in light of its educational characteristics, and to view its educational achievements in communal terms. The approach is localized, but informed by broader social and cultural developments, with an eye toward the sociological, but rooted in the particular experience and roles of key figures in the story; focused on a single century, but considered in light of the broader history of Jewish education. It is a story of real people, inspired and inspiring, foible-laden and flawed, acting amidst a complex array of social and cultural forces, forces that would ebb and flow, shift and transform, in the course of the narrative.

If in the years to come lessons learned along the way are squandered and the St. Paul Jewish community fades away, its story will be at best, like many others, a cautionary tale. But if there is a vital Jewish community in St. Paul a generation from now, it will be because the difficult lessons of previous generations were valued and continued to guide community planning. If so, other communities may draw inspiration and guidance from its story as well. In the meantime, readers may notice similarities to their own communities—similar problems, assets, and possibilities, and take the opportunity to consider what might be learned from how the St. Paul Jewish community has or has not met the challenges it has faced thus far.

The prophet Isaiah urged his disheartened community to "life your gaze skyward" and reassess current circumstances in light of eternal truths. Ultimately, however, a Jewish community's future isn't written in the stars. It is written, to the extent that it is in the hands of its members, in its schools, where learning, the definitive Jewish rite, takes place, and thus where conflicting social and ideological forces tend to converge—forces stirred by broader social influences, ambition or ideology, the presence or absence of resources, providence or disaster. Each individual is endowed with particular gifts and responsibilities, but all that the Jewish people have to offer the world, as Jews, is rooted in Jewish education. Synagogues provide a settled place for the ark of the covenant to rest, but a Jewish community's schools are the ark that moves ahead of the congregation.

Thus, a detailed consideration of this story ultimately leads back to the larger question: Why doesn't Jewish education simply fail, once and for all, at this impossible task? How to build a bridge that starts in a thousand places, spanning currents you're not sure you want to cross? And if you do want to get across, how to build the bridge and cross it at the same time? But then again, *making it across* is the oldest Jewish story and that too is the subject of this study. Part I provides a historical overview of Jewish education in St. Paul in the twentieth century. In part II, implications of lessons learned, for the St. Paul Jewish community and others, are explored.

NOTES

1. B. Talmud, *Shabbat*, 112.

2. *Mishneh Torah*, Introduction. The passage includes a paraphrase of Isaiah 29:14.

3. Jacob Marcus, ed., *The Jew in the Medieval World* (New York: Atheneum, 1973), 382. Marcus suggests that "the setting of our sun" refers to the recent death of a scholar or to the confiscation of copies of the Talmud in the area the previous year.

4. "רצינו לגדל דור של אפיקורסים, וגדלנו דור של עמי הארצות."

5. Yehudah Amichai, *Patuah, Sagur, Patuah* (Jerusalem: Schocken, 1998), 9–10.

6. Simon Rawidowicz, "Israel: The Ever Dying People," in *Studies in Jewish Thought*, N. N. Glatzer, ed. (Philadelphia: JPS, 1974), 224.

7. Arnold Dashefsky and H. M. Shapiro, *Ethnic Identification Among American Jews* (Lexington, MA: Lexington Books, 1974). Though he concurred with Dashefsky and Shapiro on this point, Steven M. Cohen appears to have overlooked their study, which is earlier than the research Cohen identifies in his "The Differential Impact of Jewish Education on Adult Jewish Identity" as the earliest research he was aware of on the topic; in *Family Matters: Jewish Education in an Age of Choice*, Jack Wertheimer, ed. (Waltham, MA: Brandeis University Press, 2007).

8. Geoffrey Bock, *Does Jewish Education Matter?* (New York: Council of Jewish Federations, 1975).

9. Harold Himmelfarb, "Jewish Education for Naught: Educating the Culturally Deprived Child," *Analysis* no. 51 (Institute for Jewish Policy Planning and Research of the Synagogue Council of America), 1–12.

10. The emergence in the Midwest of a number of leading progressive-traditionalist figures and initiatives in all of the major movements in the mid-twentieth century, including Zionist movements, is striking. Ramah in Wisconsin was the first camp in the Ramah system (1947), and Olin Sang Ruby Union Institute ("OSRUI," 1952), also in Wisconsin, was the Reform movement's first permanent camping facility. In its first several decades, the Hebrew Theological College in Chicago would prove an influential progressive force in orthodox circles. In the Twin Cities, the contested founding of United Synagogue Youth (USY) by Beth El Congregation in Minneapolis or the Temple of Aaron in St. Paul is emblematic of this salient, but one can also add the Poalei Zion *Hakhsharah* farm outside of Minneapolis (one of two in the United States), the "plain pine box" *kavod hamet* initiative begun at Adath Jeshurun Congregation, and the pioneering educational and gender egalitarian efforts of Rabbi Moses Sachs at B'nai Abraham Congregation in Minneapolis. The Twin Cities were, in fact, at the forefront of progress in the area of Jewish gender equity throughout the latter part of the twentieth century. Along with these developments, an outsized number of prominent twentieth-century Jewish scholars, educators, rabbis, artists, and communal leaders are associated with the Twin Cities, including Saadya Gelb, Albert and Max Vorspan, Moshe Goldblum, Melford Spiro, Marver Bernstein, Daniel J. Elazar, Kassel Abelson, Arnold Goodman, Bernard Raskas, Frances Butwin, Gerald Bubis, Miles Cohen, Arthur Oleisky, Moshe Feller, Jonathan Paradise, Fred Astren, Ron Keiner, Noam Zion, Jody Myers, Joel Alter, Katherine Simon, Perry Rank, Louis E. Newman, B. Elka Abrahamson, Steven Leder, Saralee Shrell-Fox, and singer-songwriter Debbie Friedman.

11. Daniel J. Elazar, *The National-Cultural Movement in Hebrew Education in the Mississippi Valley* (Jerusalem: Jerusalem Center for Public Affairs, 1993), http://www.bjpa.org/Publications/details.cfm?PublicationID=2532, Daniel Elazar On-line Library. Elazar's book *Community and Polity* carries a cryptic dedication to his aunt and uncle Rose Barzon Goldman and Samuel Goldman, who "were each a special kind of pillar of a very special community." The community Elazar alludes to was Minneapolis. His aunt's story, including her Jewish educational work in Minneapolis

and St. Paul, is lovingly recounted in the "Personal Note" appended to "The National-Cultural Movement in Hebrew Education in the Mississippi Valley."

12. In the 1995 edition of *Community and Polity*, Elazar briefly reiterates and updates his previous observations about St. Paul and Minneapolis, but the St. Paul population figures he uses would soon be revised upward by approximately a third. A 1981 Fund and Council sponsored population study (http://databank.bjpa.org/Studies/details.cfm?StudyID=466) arrived at an upper estimate of 7,689, while a 1993 Fund and Council study (http://databank.bjpa.org/Studies/details.cfm?StudyID=384) put the number at approximately 10,000, not counting a sizable number of individuals "who identified with non-Jewish religions" but were related to a Jewish member of the household. Elazar also appeared to have misunderstood the relationship between the Talmud Torah of St. Paul's supplementary and day school programs.

Part I

Chapter 1

How Far Is It from the Banks of the Jordan to the Banks of the Mississippi?

Greater St. Paul, Minnesota, stretches along a bend on the Upper Mississippi, adjacent to neighboring Minneapolis to the west. Ancient burial mounds overlook the winding river gorge. The mounds, begun long before Dakotah villages were established in the area 300 to 400 years ago, bear witness to the enduring power of the Mississippi to draw pilgrims and settlers to its bluffs. Euro-American settlement of the area began in the early nineteenth century, stimulated by the fur trade and the establishment of Fort Snelling at the nearby intersection of the Mississippi and Minnesota Rivers. A riverboat landing soon followed, around which the town of St. Paul quickly expanded. Shortly after Minnesota became a state in 1858, St. Paul was designated the state capitol, and in the years that followed, it would also become a major railroad hub. Though infected with the same racism and bigotry found elsewhere in the United States, European Americans, African Americans, and Dakotah would live side by side along the river for several decades.[1] However, Dakotah resistance to mounting encroachment and dispossession, culminating in the United States-Dakotah War of 1862, would lead to the destruction of Dakotah settlements in the area, and the imprisonment and subsequent banishment of the survivors to reservations outside of Minnesota. Thus, the foundations of St. Paul, like so many other cities, ages past and present, were laid amid the ruins of an exiled people.

By 1900 the city had grown to 163,000 residents. Though smaller than Minneapolis, St. Paul would become the hometown of a remarkable array of public figures and ethnic communities; a city of vigorous, civic-oriented Catholicism and strong labor unions, including a prominent chapter of the Brotherhood of Sleeping Car Porters, which would play an important role in the development of a vibrant African American community; a city of conservative cultures and progressive politics; the home of "Morgan's

11

Mexican-Lebanese Foods" on the city's West Side, owned and operated by the Jewish Permuth family, a proud nod to four ethnic communities settled in adjacent neighborhoods, wrapped around one corner store. Historians commonly note that unlike Minneapolis, the relative unimportance of a relocated New England elite in St. Paul in its formative years made it a more welcoming and secure place for communities more severely marginalized in other locales. A generous share of prohibition era, crime-related notoriety did little to dim its liberal profile, the title of Carey McWilliams's 1946 exposé of anti-Semitism in Minneapolis, "Minneapolis: The Curious Twin," alluding to comparatively less overt anti-Semitism across the river in St. Paul.[2]

The city's diverse social and cultural history can be read in the names of prominent figures that hailed from the city, including F. Scott Fitzgerald, Roy Wilkins, Whitney Young, Gordon Parks, Kate Millet, and Harry Blackmun.[3] These factors also contributed to an enriched intellectual environment for St. Paul youth. In the first half of the twentieth century, eleven future Rhode Scholars graduated from St. Paul Central High School, more than any other high school in the country, and St. Paul remains today second only to Boston in the number of institutions of higher learning per capita within its city limits.[4]

Jews have lived in the vicinity since the mid-1800s, though the first documented use of Hebrew in the area was not among Jews, but rather in the form of a Hebrew-Dakotah dictionary composed by Presbyterian missionary Gideon Pond in 1834.[5] In 1856, two years before the State of Minnesota was established, a small group of German-speaking Jews formed Mt. Zion Hebrew Association, St. Paul's first Jewish congregation. Its founding immediately gave rise to a short-lived dissenting group bearing the ironic name "*Ahabath Achim*/Brotherly Love," followed by several other congregations in the ensuing decades.[6] By 1900, approximately 5000 Jews lived in the city.

St. Paul continued to have a larger Jewish population than Minneapolis through the end of the century; however, by 1880 Minneapolis had become the bigger of the two cities, spurred on by its emergence as a world center for grain milling,[7] and by 1910 it had a larger Jewish population as well.[8] Nevertheless, St. Paul's Jewish population continued to grow, reaching its peak in the 1930s at approximately 14,000.[9]

The earliest Jewish neighborhoods, swelled by the arrival of Eastern European emigrants fleeing anti-Jewish restrictions and violence, poverty, and war, formed on the edges of downtown and along the river flats of St. Paul's "lower West Side," far below the ancient mounds on the surrounding bluffs. Neighborhood institutions soon followed, including a piecemeal array of "afternoon," or "supplementary" Jewish schools.[10] Recognizing the opportunities access to the American mainstream could provide, these schools ceded the greater part of the day to public school education, while claiming seven to ten hours a week, on weekday afternoons and Sunday mornings, for Jewish studies.[11]

Figure 1.1   The Hebrew Institute/*Hakhnasat Or'him* (Shelter Home) Building, 1912.
Source: Berman Upper Midwest Jewish Archives, University of Minnesota Libraries.

During the St. Paul's community's first hundred years, formal education for Jewish youth would be offered almost entirely through these supplementary schools, or, in the case of Mt. Zion Congregation, which was offering a formal educational program by the early 1870s, by way of a Reform-style "Sabbath" [Sunday] school.[12] The new building of the more traditional Sons of Jacob Congregation on College Avenue, completed in 1881, included instructional space. The congregation was soon offering its own supplementary program, the forerunner of the Capital City Free Hebrew School,[13] while on the West Side, the Hebrew Institute, founded in 1911, shared space with the Jewish Sheltering Home, a *hakhnasat or'him* residence for indigent and transient Jews (Figures 1.1 and 1.2).

Though rooted in very real ideological and geographic divides, a growing bric-a-brac of supplementary programs would come to be seen as problematic by Jewish educational reformers in the city, leading to periodic calls for consolidation of educational programs to meet the challenge of equitable and effective allocation of community resources. But the concerns ran deeper than the need for greater efficiency. Pious myths about the Jewish acumen of previous generations notwithstanding, a study of Jewish education in the city in 1935,

Figure 1.2   The Capital City Free Hebrew School, c. 1920. The words "Talmud Torah" appear over the doorways of both the Capital City School and the Hebrew Institute (Figure 1.1). *Source*: Berman Upper Midwest Jewish Archives, University of Minnesota Libraries.

as its Jewish population was reaching its peak, estimated that the majority of Jewish youth in St. Paul were receiving no formal Jewish education at all.[14]

These concerns would also be stirred by broader trends in Jewish intellectual circles. As communal leaders in St. Paul grappled with local issues, influential voices in Europe and North America were calling for greater attention to mounting educational disarray. Fruitful engagement with the challenges and opportunities of changing social conditions, they argued, required the placement of schools, rather than synagogues, at the center of communal life. In a 1907 address on "The Jewish Primary School," Jewish Theological Seminary professor Louis Ginzberg insisted that placing communal educational institutions at the center of Jewish life, far from an innovation, was a reaffirmation of a traditional value structure, in that in previous generations, "the Jews met their ideal saint outside of the synagogue as well as inside. He was a thinking and an acting saint no less than a praying saint." Recovering this sensibility, Ginzberg concluded, was of utmost importance: "If Jewish education is to resume its old place and significance in Jewish life, it must cease to be the supernumerary adjunct of a person or a cause. It must again be an independent institution, fulfilling its task autonomously. It must be, as it was, the focus of Jewish life, of the Jewish intellect, and of the Jewish religion."[15]

Efforts to establish a central educational institution in St. Paul coincided with these developments. In 1918, along with initial planning for the construction of a Jewish community recreation center, a chapter of the Young Men's Hebrew Association, similar to the YMCA in its focus on positive recreational programming, was formed in St. Paul.[16] The following year these recreation-oriented efforts were linked with communal educational goals when the local B'nai B'rith chapter put forward an unsuccessful plan for a combined community center and central community school.[17] Founders of the Jewish Educational Center and Hebrew School, established in the early 1930s, also intended this role for the institution, but its joint administration of educational and recreational functions was short-lived, the two wings of the Center becoming separate associations in 1934.[18] The name "Center School" would endure, but persistent divisions in the community, physical and philosophical, would prevent the school from fulfilling the role of a central educational-recreational agency for the community as a whole.[19]

In the 1940s, as the scale of devastation suffered by the Jews of Europe became ever clearer and identification with the Zionist vision of rescue and national renewal in Palestine grew stronger, new leadership emerged in St. Paul with a vigorous communal agenda, and calls for educational consolidation were renewed. In 1945 Dan Rosenberg was hired as executive director of the recently consolidated St. Paul United Jewish Fund and Council (UJFC), a position he would hold through the mid-1960s. Rosenberg is often singled out as having been a particularly able advocate for communal agencies in the post–World War II period. Kokie Goldenberg, a local businessman and active participant in several communal initiatives in the 1940s and 1950s, recalled that not long after becoming Fund and Council director, Rosenberg mentioned that he had been reviewing minutes of past UJFC board meetings and was struck by how much of its time was taken up with educational issues. It wasn't long, as Goldenberg remembered it, before Rosenberg had organized a committee to respond to the accumulating concerns.[20] This, apparently, was the origin of a Fund and Council "Social Planning Committee," which recommended the founding of a communal body to coordinate education programs in the city.[21] The resulting agency, the St. Paul Bureau of Jewish Education (BJE), was established in 1948,[22] under the aegis of the Fund and Council. The bureau's board of directors was made up of twelve members named by each of the participating schools, twelve appointed by the Fund and Council and the community's congregational rabbis. A merger of the Center-Capital Hebrew School and the recently established Kaplan Hebrew Seminary, named for local businessman and philanthropist George Kaplan and initially aligned with the Hebrew Institute, immediately followed, the new school taking on the name "Bureau of Jewish Education."[23] The only other remaining supplementary program, the West Side's Hebrew Institute, where Yiddish continued to be the language of instruction and "old-world" methods and attitudes continued to prevail, would agree only to a tentative association with the bureau.[24]

The Hebrew Institute would draw its waning student body from the shrinking West Side neighborhood, while the newly consolidated BJE's students came mostly from neighborhoods north and west of downtown.[25]

Unlike the Hebrew Institute, the Bureau School would employ innovative educational techniques, including a Hebrew-in-Hebrew (*iv'rit b'iv'rit*) language instruction curriculum,[26] with supplementary instruction in English. Such methods had been pioneered at the turn of the century in Europe by the *heder m'tukan* movement,[27] and in the United States by Samson Benderly, Mordecai Kaplan, and their circle of progressive educators based at the Teachers Institute of the Conservative movement's Jewish Theological Seminary. Associated innovations, including an emphasis on student well-being and classroom aesthetics, were brought to St. Paul by Rabbi Philip Kleinman and his niece Anna Kleinman (Schwartz), who came to St. Paul to assist her uncle. Kleinman had been a member of the Benderly group before accepting the position of rabbi at the Temple of Aaron in 1917, and during his ten years in St. Paul would prove a forceful advocate of innovation in education and liturgy[28] (Figure 1.3).

Figure 1.3   Rabbi Philip Kleinman, Anna Kleinman (Schwartz), and a 1917–1918 Temple of Aaron Class. *Source:* Berman Upper Midwest Jewish Archives, University of Minnesota Libraries.

Kleinman's and niece Anna's educational perspectives were informed by concurrent experimentation with the "education center" model in New York. Though his efforts were limited at first to the Temple of Aaron Hebrew School, Kleinman envisioned the formation of a communal educational center in St. Paul as well. In his last year at the Temple of Aaron (1926), the semi-independent Temple of Aaron Community Hebrew School was established, a Midwestern offshoot of the "educational center" model. The Jewish Education Center and Hebrew School (1930), the merged Jewish Education Center—Capital City School (1933–1944), and the BJE School would each, in turn, be strongly influenced by this vision. The title "Jewish Bureau of Education," in St. Paul and elsewhere, was itself a link to Benderly's pioneering "Bureau of Education," established in conjunction with the New York "Kehillah" initiative to bring order and efficiency to the city's Jewish institutions and programs through an integrated communal administrative structure.[29] Following his departure, Kleinman's legacy was sustained and extended by coworker and successor Louis Gordon, whose efforts formed a living bridge between the introduction of a progressive, communal approach to Jewish education in St. Paul in the early years of the century, and the establishment of the BJE thirty years later.[30]

An editorial published in the June 4, 1948, edition of the *American Jewish World* lauded the success of the Fund and Council's "planning committee" in establishing a BJE in St. Paul (Figure 1.4). This process, resulting in a "unified plan for Jewish education in the community," indicated that St. Paul was moving beyond admiration, to emulation of the Minneapolis community's exceptionally successful collaborative educational model. The day might not be far distant, the editorial concluded, "when the dream of decades will be realized."[31] In the postwar years, enrollments at the Bureau school would surge, with the student body rising from 186 students in 1951 to approximately 500 in 1953. At the same time, enrollments at the West Side's Hebrew Institute continued to dwindle.[32] By the early 1950s, only 12 percent of St. Paul's approximately 12,000 Jews lived on the West Side.[33] The long decline of the neighborhood, hastened by repeated flooding of the river flats, catalyzed efforts to consolidate educational programs. However, as attention began to focus on the construction of a new building to house the communal educational agency, the bureau struggled to extend its mandate beyond the recently merged Kaplan Seminary and Center-Capital City supplementary programs.[34] George Kaplan had actively championed the construction of a communal educational facility for the newly unified school, going so far as to announce an initial pledge of $100,000 toward its construction at the 1949 meeting of the National Association for Jewish Education.[35] Nevertheless, as the bureau, heartened by his offer, moved to consolidate the remaining educational programs, the tenuous network of organizations and congregations it had assembled began to unravel. The perceived advantages of coordinated educational programming had prompted the formation of the bureau, but that perception alone was proving insufficient for realizing its mandate. A "Community school" implied a community effort, and as would soon become apparent, attitudes about the particulars of the project fell far short of consensus (Figure 1.4).

Wrapping the effort around the initiative of a single benefactor had, itself, proven a problem, as Kaplan's pledge simultaneously stimulated support and opposition. This issue was further exacerbated when, having initially indicated that the new school would be built at the intersection of Randolph Avenue and Macalester Street, at some distance from any synagogue building, the BJE instead accepted an offer of land once again belonging to a single benefactor—this time a member of the Temple of Aaron—adjacent to a new Temple of Aaron building on Mississippi River Boulevard.[36] An unsigned memorandum prepared for the Board and Building Commission

Figure 1.4   Document Signing to Establish the St. Paul Bureau of Jewish Education. Dan Rosenberg, executive director of the St. Paul United Jewish Fund and Council, is seated on the far right, George Kaplan, representing the Kaplan Hebrew Seminary, is in the middle. *Source*: Berman Upper Midwest Jewish Archives, University of Minnesota Libraries.

of the BJE regarding the logistical advantages of the site conveys a clear understanding of the larger issues associated with the location, including support among members of the Temple of Aaron for a congregational school of its own. In responding to this challenge, the memorandum focuses on the importance of sustaining the public character of a communal school. Under the subheading "Community School Versus Congregational School" the author, most likely Harry Rosenthal, chair of the BJE's Building Committee, asserted:

> There is a segment in the Temple of Aaron who feel that the place of a Talmud Torah is in the Synagogue and that the new Synagogue structure should house either a three or a five-day-a-week congregational school. An amalgamation would forever obviate the possibility of ever having a congregational school. I feel that it is right that it be so. Education, I mean general secular education, is the responsibility of the entire community. People who have no children attending public school pay taxes towards our school system so that the children of others may obtain education. I believe it is unwise and undesirable for a Synagogue [*sic*] to take that responsibility away from the community.[37]

As audacious as the assertion that Jewish education ought to emulate the model of public responsibility for public schools might appear, Kokie Goldenberg, who would hold a number of prominent positions in the community, and at the time served as president of the United Fund and Council, would later recall having advocated for such a system as well.[38]

The memorandum clearly reflected a very real inclination toward collaboration. At roughly the same time, Mt. Zion, its budget strained by the cost of its own new building, had approached the bureau about assuming responsibility for its religious school. That the community's Reform congregation would even inquire about such a possibility suggests a broadly shared sense of common purpose underlying the BJE's work—though not broad enough, as the request was turned down, on the grounds that a Reform curriculum was "educationally unsound."[39]

While the bureau was fielding Mt. Zion's request, it was also at loggerheads with Orthodox supporters of the much-diminished Hebrew Institute, who decried the decision to locate the planned community school next to the new home of the Conservative—affiliated Temple of Aaron. These critics maintained that funds had been solicited for the project with the understanding that the school would be located at the more neutral Macalester and Randolph site, but that at a dubious meeting between bureau representatives and Temple of Aaron board members late in 1953, a "deal" had been reached to build the building adjacent to the synagogue. Placing a "community school" next to the Temple of Aaron, the dissenters argued, signaled Conservative domination of the agency and abandonment of traditional Jewish learning and practice.[40] Such critics of the move could certainly avail themselves of a worrisome precedent. The Temple of Aaron Community Hebrew School, the Jewish Education Center School, and the merged Center-Capital City School, though ostensibly communal successors to the Temple of Aaron's congregational school, had also been located adjacent to the Temple of Aaron at the Holly and Grotto site, and were commonly viewed as remaining within the congregation's orbit.

Efforts continued to coordinate and strengthen educational programs in the community, including an agreement between the bureau and Mount Zion, the Temple of Aaron, and Sons of Jacob congregations to form a community-wide teacher's placement bureau and to work toward greater consistency in curricula.[41] Nevertheless, as construction of the facility progressed, charges of biased committees and broken promises continued to be exchanged. At one point, Hebrew Institute supporters went so far as to seek a united front with Reform—affiliated Mt. Zion Congregation against Conservative domination of the new school,[42] while at the same time charging that an expected shortening of the school week from five to four days (Sunday mornings reverting to the congregations) evidenced anti-orthodox duplicity.[43] In a statement drafted by the Rabbi of Sons of Jacob Congregation Morris, Casriel Katz, the Hebrew Institute Board asserted, "Sunday Schools are to be more and more exploited for the expansion of Conservative and Reform temples to help ease the great financial burdens of their vast building projects—at the expense of the Talmud Torah."[44] In a subsequent letter to the editor of the American Jewish World, Katz would lay claim to the very title "Talmud Torah," concluding, "The Hebrew Institute Talmud Torah wants to continue as a Talmud Torah of real traditional Judaism. It is asking for the same right to live and be supported by the Jewish Community as the Bureau Hebrew School."[45]

Backers of the new agency nevertheless remained resolute. In a move that would have long-term consequences for the community, the Fund and Council, increasingly representative of the community's non-orthodox households and institutions, responded to Hebrew Institute supporters' resistance to the plan by discontinuing its allocation, on the grounds that it was not cooperating "with other such agencies in preventing duplication of effort and in promoting efficiency and economy of administration."[46]

The struggle to fashion a communal educational agency would stand at the center of the St. Paul community's efforts to reconstruct itself. It was a struggle shaped by local history, interests, and personalities, but as Daniel Elazar argued, the ultimate success of those efforts is best understood in the context of a larger, regional narrative. Before returning to subsequent developments in St. Paul, a closer look at nearby communities will help to establish that context.

JEWISH EDUCATION IN MINNEAPOLIS
AND DULUTH-SUPERIOR

St. Paul's difficulties establishing a central educational agency were especially exasperating, given that the model to emulate was just across the river. The American Jewish World had noted as much in its coverage of the founding of the St. Paul BJE. The Talmud Torah of Minneapolis had been established in 1914 as an "educational and recreational agency,"[47] as would the St. Paul Jewish Education Center and Hebrew School several years later.[48] However, unlike supplementary programs in St. Paul and most other communities around the country, in the middle decades of the century the Talmud Torah of Minneapolis rapidly rose to a singular, preeminent position—"a community jewel" among Minneapolis Jewish institutions[49]—above the competitive reach of the city's congregations.[50] The school would quickly come to embody characteristics associated with Benderly's vision of the Jewish communal supplementary school.

Writing in 1920, Isaac Berkson, a member of Benderly's circle, maintained, "Consistent with this conception the [Talmud Torah], as the Communal Jewish School is called, becomes the central agency of the community, the institution around which it builds the social life and by means of which it transmits the significant culture of the ethnic group."[51] From the 1920s through the mid-1970s the Talmud Torah of Minneapolis would occupy the central position in Minneapolis Jewish life that Berkson envisioned. The long association of local physician Dr. George Gordon with the school had resulted in the development of an inclusive and progressive school ethos. Under Gordon's guidance, the Minneapolis Talmud Torah would attract an able faculty, and prove fertile ground for labor Zionist activism, enhancing its profile as a relevant and dynamic presence in the community. Years earlier, Gordon had been instrumental in transforming the school's predecessor institution from an Eastern-European-style *heder* to a progressive communal educational agency. By 1922, its new building on Eighth Avenue and Fremont on the city's North Side included a swimming pool and gymnasium, and the school had accrued a wide array of social service and cultural functions. Such developments were in keeping with the "educational center" model advocated by Benderly and Berkson, and guiding Kleinman's efforts in St. Paul. Gordon, however, expressed concern that the educational focus of the institution not be overwhelmed by other functions. In a letter to Benderly's associate Mordecai Kaplan prior to the addition of the swimming pool, Gordon had shared his worry that a pool would "drown the Talmud Torah,"[52] and in 1924 the institution's educational unit was separated from its accompanying social functions. The educational and social functions of the St. Paul Jewish Education Center would likewise be separated a few years later, resulting in independent "Community Centers" in both cities.

Once again focused on its educational mission, the Minneapolis Talmud Torah underwent a period of remarkable growth. Gordon remained its guiding figure and his prestige, the result of his devotion to communal causes, his work as a physician, his unassailable integrity, and emergence as a representative figure in the larger community ensured the school's continued preeminence, even after his death in 1943.[53] The Talmud Torah's unrivaled position as the community's central educational institution and, as such, the only supplementary program to receive funding from the Minneapolis Federation, was attributable, to a large degree, to his efforts and influence. As long as the Minneapolis community sustained Gordon's vision of the Talmud Torah as communal common ground, the level of learning and degree of social integration it provided would prove impressive.

A 1957 study of Jewish education in Minneapolis, commissioned by the Minneapolis Federation and authored by Louis L. Ruffman, confirmed the Talmud Torah's distinguished status. The study recommended expanding its role in the community even further by becoming more directly involved in training teachers, assisting synagogue programs with curriculum development and Hebrew instruction, helping with inter-school programming, developing a community arts program, and enhancing adult education programming. Ruffman concluded:

> It is clear that all of the synagogue schools functioning in the community can profit greatly by a community-sponsored program of educational guidance. Such a program is usually provided by a central Bureau of Jewish Education. Such central agencies have developed a wide range of services which can be used by all types of schools functioning in the community. There is, however, no need nor would, it be desirable, to set up a separate agency for this purpose in Minneapolis, since the Talmud Torah is, in effect, already a community-sponsored agency by virtue of the fact that it receives almost its entire budget from the general community. To meet the existing need, therefore, it is strongly recommended that the functions of the Talmud Torah be broadened so that it can serve as a central agency offering educational guidance to the other schools functioning in the community, and meeting certain other educational needs of the community as a whole.[54]

In its ascendency, the Talmud Torah of Minneapolis was perhaps the single most successful example of Benderly's vision of progressive Jewish communal education in the country—though it happened to be a thousand miles west of Manhattan. Philip Kleinman and Louis Gordon in St. Paul, and George Gordon in Minneapolis were all quite familiar with developments in Jewish education further East, and were in contact with central figures in those efforts. While others struggled to establish such institutions in what seemed, at the time, more likely locales, something unexpected was unfolding on the Upper Mississippi. So strong had been the Talmud Torah's position in the community up until this point that it was common for Orthodox-affiliated Torah Academy day school students to attend the Talmud Torah as well.[55]

The loss of this recognition as the community's central and preeminent educational institution would come with a successful effort by Temple Israel, a large, long-standing Reform congregation on the city's South Side, to secure community funding for its supplementary school. This congregation-based challenge to the communal mission of the agency would be one of many centrifugal developments in Minneapolis in the last third of the century. Increasing disassociation of orthodox segments of the community, who had previously been active partners in the Talmud Torah, would exacerbate the situation. By the end of the century, support had largely evaporated and was replaced by an increasingly insular orthodox orientation. The eventual dissolution of the Minneapolis Talmud Torah's privileged position in the community would signal broader communal disarray and educational decline.

Though significantly smaller than the Minneapolis and St. Paul communities, mid-century Duluth-Superior, the third largest Jewish population center in the area, would exhibit similar tendencies. Louis Gordon would provide a personal link between the communities, serving as a Jewish educator in Superior before beginning his long and influential tenure in St. Paul.[56] Findings of a 1944 study of the Duluth community's "social, recreational and educational" characteristics, authored by Leo Honor (an early member of the Benderly-Mordecai Kaplan circle) and Elias Picheny, suggested an educational environment quite similar to St. Paul, in particular. At the time of the study, Duluth had two educational programs, one offered by the Reform Congregation and the alternative associated with the community's other three congregations, identified as "Orthodox." The latter program was formally designated the "Hebrew Institute," but was commonly referred to as the "Talmud Torah." Unlike St. Paul's "Hebrew Institute," the Duluth Hebrew Institute offered an *ivrit-b'ivrit* curriculum, with Israel Pollack's child-centered Hebrew primer *Sifri* already in use in the 1930s. Like other settings around the country, Honor and Picheny's study indicated that approximately half of community's children were receiving no Jewish education "under organized auspices," but the institute, attended by about half of the children enrolled in a Jewish educational program in Duluth, "in comparison to other such institutions in the country, is attracting children at a younger age and is keeping them longer in school."[57] Fifty-seven percent of its budget came from the Jewish Welfare Federation, 10 percent from tuition, and the remainder from gifts, rental of space, and support from its Sisterhood. The authors emphasized the importance of building on the Talmud Torah's strengths to more effectively reach out beyond its devoted base, along with the development of citywide social and cultural programming in cooperation with the Reform Congregation, to "give all the children a feeling of belonging to one community, regardless of religious affiliations and home background."[58]

In 1954, the Duluth Talmud Torah, now housed in the Jewish Educational Center (once again, a combined educational, recreation and cultural center), would be renamed the Ida B. Cook Hebrew School, in honor of an early educational leader in the community. One indication of its continued prominence was the attendance of approximately 200 community members, out of a total Jewish population of 2,500 at a banquet held in 1955 to celebrate the fiftieth anniversary of the agency and its predecessor schools.

Reflection on the ironic possibility that Benderly and Kaplan-inspired educational reforms might be better suited to mid-size, Midwestern locales than to the cities in which they originated was slow in coming. The most prominent chroniclers of Jewish education in the United States, with the exception of Daniel Elazar and Arnold Dashefsky, though aware of developments in the Twin Cities, tended to go no further than allude to unexpected successes in unlikely places. Jacob R. Marcus, commenting in 1993 on the Talmud Torah of Minneapolis's national reputation, which he attributed primarily to the efforts of George Gordon, added that it was "curious" that this had occurred, given that the school was "off by itself, distant from mass Jewish communities," but he didn't go on to consider the possibility that the location of this success was more than a curiosity.[59] In his introduction to *Jewish Education in the United States, A Documentary History*, Lloyd Gartner briefly referenced several locations outside of New York, including Minneapolis, where local educators "led Hebrew schooling in their cities, federating the schools and raising standards." Gartner went on to suggest that the size of the communities had proven an asset in these efforts, but left the more "curious" questions regarding these communities unanswered, concluding, "With far smaller and more cohesive Jewish communities than in New York, it was a good deal easier to found bureaus of Jewish education and adjust educational facilities to local needs. Moreover, the local federations of Jewish philanthropies proved somewhat more amenable to assisting Jewish education."[60]

Though brief, Gartner's comments did suggest that there might be something to learn from what seemed an unlikely setting for success. A pair of articles appearing in the *Journal of Jewish Education* in the fall of 1982 by longtime Minneapolis Talmud Torah administrators L. I. Kaiser and Mordecai Sochen took Gartner's observations a bit further. Though neither discussed Jewish education in neighboring St. Paul—Kaiser betrays a typical note of condescension toward St. Paul in his article—Kaiser in particular went beyond repeating often-heard accolades to considering *why* "at national or regional educational conferences, the reaction was always: 'Minneapolis שאני,' 'Minneapolis is different.'"[61] Acknowledging that there might be some truth to the claim that there was a regional aspect to this distinction, related "to our remoteness from the East, the source of Jewish social and cultural chaos and confusion," Kaiser went on to list and comment upon three additional factors: the geography of the community, excellent leadership, and excellent teachers.[62]

The significance of Kaiser's observations is not limited to his conclusions. Perhaps of greater importance is the underlying assertion that the common observation that Minneapolis was "different" warranted a closer look, and that what one saw upon looking more closely was a mix of factors, some of which were within the control of the community (leadership and teachers), while others were "givens" (location and local geography).

Meanwhile, just across the Mississippi, a few miles closer to Benderly and Mordecai Kaplan's New York City, the story seemed, in some respects, reversed. A far less congenial process had taken hold in smaller, more tradition-bound St. Paul. It would eventually lead to the establishment of a central educational agency there as well, though at first efforts aimed at greater educational cooperation appeared to generate more heat than light. St. Paul would prove a more contentious and pedagogically old-world environment, lacking a figure comparable to Minneapolis's George Gordon, who had so compellingly personified the virtues of a central educational institution.[63] It was the home of well-regarded Jewish educators, most notably Louis Gordon (no relation to George Gordon). However, no educator in St. Paul enjoyed the broad and deep esteem afforded Minneapolis's Gordon. Nevertheless, as the reputation of the Talmud Torah of Minneapolis was peaking, the advantages of a communal educational agency in St. Paul were becoming ever more apparent as well.

THE TALMUD TORAH OF ST. PAUL

The Duluth Talmud Torah's fiftieth anniversary celebration and the publication of the Ruffman report on the Talmud Torah of Minneapolis both came within a year of the establishment of the Talmud Torah of St. Paul and the dedication of the George Kaplan Education Building, its new home.

The title "Talmud Torah" had long been used in Europe to indicate a communally organized and administered school, typically serving the community's poorer children, as distinct from a "*heder*/room," so-named because it often met in one of the rooms of the teacher's home, though in the United States the two terms were commonly used interchangeably. Similarly, "Talmud Torah" had been used to describe one or another of St. Paul's supplementary schools for decades. Both the Capital City Hebrew School and the Hebrew Institute had "Talmud Torah" in Hebrew letters over their front entryways. *"Talmud Torah d'St. Paul"* appeared at the top of the Capital City Hebrew School report card, above "Capital City Hebrew School" in English, and the Hebrew Institute would continue to be referred to as the "Hebrew Institute Talmud Torah" through the 1950s.[64] Following the lead of the Talmud Torah of Minneapolis/Minneapolis Talmud Torah, "St. Paul Talmud Torah"[65] would replace "St. Paul Bureau of Jewish Education" as the name of the agency, coinciding with the opening of the new facility on Mississippi River Boulevard.[66]

With the founding of the Talmud Torah, the St. Paul BJE would be dissolved. Unlike in many other locations, where bureaus of Jewish education—also often termed "central educational agencies"—struggled to impose a degree of consistency and accountability on their constituents from above (as had the St. Paul Bureau), the Talmud Torah of St. Paul, like the Talmud Torah of Minneapolis, would itself function as a central agency for the community, in the form of a single, unified community school. That these two communities were so constituted as to allow for such an arrangement would contribute enormously to the success of both institutions. Veteran Jewish educator Meyer Gallin was appointed the Talmud Torah of St. Paul's first executive director, as well as executive director of the more loosely organized "St. Paul Association for Jewish Education" (SPAJE), a local branch of the National Association for Jewish Education.[67] Gallin's appointment and groundbreaking for the new facility, scheduled to open in the fall of 1956, signaled a firm resolve on the part of the Fund and Council to proceed with a coordinated educational plan.

Tensions would eventually subside. Fund and Council director Rosenberg is often credited with playing a key role in shepherding the project to completion. His influence, however, was undoubtedly enhanced by a widespread inclination, shared by Fund and Council leaders, to identify communal agencies with the long-term interests of the community as a whole.

Along with substantive signs of progress toward greater cooperation, one could observe symbolic indications of progress as well. After voicing bitter disappointment with the process leading to its establishment, Rabbi Morris Casriel Katz nonetheless accepted the honor of leading the *"Sheheyiyanu"* at the laying of the cornerstone of the George Kaplan Education Building, the agency's new home, in June of 1956. Benjamin Silman, Rabbi of the Gedalia Leib Synagogue,[68] also an orthodox congregation, gave the invocation, while Ellen (Nellie) Greenberg, who along with her husband Phil had been an active supporter of Jewish education in the community, was given the honor of laying the cornerstone, as George Kaplan and Harry Rosenthal, chair of the Building Committee, looked on (Figure 1.5).

Figure 1.5　George Kaplan Education Building Cornerstone Ceremony, June 1956.
George Kaplan and Nellie Greenberg. *Source*: Berman Upper Midwest Jewish Archives,
University of Minnesota Libraries.

The *American Jewish World* article on the occasion carried the headline
"People of Vision See Dream Fulfilled at St. Paul T. T. Corner-stone Laying,"
and Janet Kroll began her coverage of the event with an allusion to the great
rivers of Jewish history:

> How far is it from the Banks of the Jordan to the rivers of Babylon, from the
> shores of the Tiber and Volga to the banks of the Mississippi?
> Only as far as men and women with vision can carry along with them genera-
> tion after generation of sons and daughters who will follow in their footsteps
> through time and space.[69]

The formal dedication of the school would follow in October, 100 years
after the founding of Mt. Zion, St. Paul's first synagogue. Ira Eisenstein, a
leader of the Reconstructionist movement and son-in-law of Mordecai Kaplan,
was the featured speaker for the occasion.[70] At both the cornerstone ceremony
and the dedication, the multi-program character of the agency would be

Figure 1.6   Talmud Torah of St. Paul Dedication Ceremony, October 1956. l–r: Ira Eisenstein, George Kaplan, Eleanor Kaplan, Irwine Gordon. *Source*: Minnesota Historical Society Archives.

emphasized, with the early childhood program as well as the supplementary school figuring prominently on both occasions (Figures 1.6 and 1.7).

By the end of the decade George Kaplan had died, the Hebrew Institute had closed its doors, and the St. Paul Association for Jewish Education, after backtracking on the cooperative agreements reached among the congregations prior to the opening of the Talmud Torah, would also soon be disbanded. However, the principal accomplishment of the BJE/SPAJE, securing the Talmud Torah's position in the community, would prove a crucial step toward effective community-wide educational collaboration. Unlike in many other locations around the country in the 1940s and 1950s, where the view that Jewish education was a communal responsibility was largely displaced by a shift to congregation and movement-based programs, in St. Paul establishing an integrated communal educational structure had moved to the center of Fund and Council priorities. Vestigial misunderstanding of the nature of the new agency would persist in some quarters, but support for the Talmud Torah as a communal institution was clearly growing, as exemplified by an incident at a final budget meeting of the United Fund and Council in the

Figure 1.7 Talmud Torah Preschool Dedication, October 1956. Dale Harris, director
of the University of Minnesota Child Welfare Institute; Molly Weiller, in whose husband
Henry's honor the preschool was dedicated; Shirley Smith, preschool director. *Source*:
Minnesota Historical Society Archives.

early 1960s. At the meeting, a board member moved that the Talmud Torah
receive no allocation at all, characterizing the agency as a private school, to
be supported by those who required its services. At this point, board member
Al Heller rose to speak against the motion, asserting that though his children
didn't need the services of the Talmud Torah, the *community* needed them,
and that he would therefore move that the Talmud Torah receive its *full*
request, a rare occurrence at the time. A participant in the meeting recalled
that the vote strongly affirmed Heller's motion, a clear indication of broad
support among the members of the Fund and Council board of directors for
the Talmud Torah as a communal institution.[71]

By 1963, Talmud Torah enrollment had reached approximately 550 students, before dropping to around 450 students in 1968.[72] As the new school
took root, it became clear that the misgivings of Hebrew Institute supporters
about its likely embrace of modern methods and curricula were well founded.
Though Yiddish had remained the language of instruction at the Hebrew
Institute through the 1940s, and the Talmud Torah would initially inherit
some faculty members with similar loyalties and inclinations, the new school

would adopt a Hebrew-in-Hebrew (*iv'rit b'ivrit*) language curriculum with supplementary instruction in English, with common expectations and opportunities for boys and girls. Along with the influence of Samson Benderly and his circle, reforms advocated by "Cultural-Zionist" thinkers such as Ahad Haam and other progressive figures in the Conservative movement would exert a decisive influence on the school's structure, curriculum, and methods. In the years ahead, positions at the Talmud Torah would be increasingly filled by similarly inclined Jewish educators, now also schooled in Dewey, Schwab, Piaget, and Bruner.

In addition to the social, cultural, and financial virtues of communal rather than congregation-based schools, the arrangement had important curricular implications as well. Freed of direct responsibility for liturgical training for bar and bat mitzvah celebrations, a community school was in a position to embrace broader and deeper educational goals. Conversely, focusing educational energies and resources in communal schools allowed congregations to concentrate their own efforts on liturgical skills. This division of labor, far from undermining liturgical education, had the potential to stimulate education effectiveness in both settings, as was evidenced by the development of highly innovative and successful liturgical skills programs at all four Twin Cities Conservative Congregations in the 1960s and 1970s.

The appointment in 1969 of Harry Malin as the Talmud Torah's fourth executive director would prove a turning point, administratively and pedagogically. Malin was a graduate of the Jewish Theological Seminary's Teachers Institute (led by Mordecai Kaplan) and a seasoned Jewish educator. Two short-term executive directors had followed Meyer Gallin, and at the end of the 1960s, ostensibly to provide additional time for synagogue programming, the school moved from a four-day-week-plus Sunday schedule to a two-day-a-week program, plus optional Sunday morning classes for elementary students.[73] Nevertheless, during Malin's tenure the school would come to be seen as a mature agency in its own right, marked by growing professionalization of the faculty and expansion of the curriculum.[74] His term would end abruptly, largely at the prompting of faculty members who, according to an AAJE (American Association for Jewish Education) report that accompanied his departure, though generally pleased with the direction of the school, were unhappy with his handling of particular personnel matters.[75] Nevertheless, Dashefsky and Shapiro, in their study of Jewish life in St. Paul, writing at the midpoint in Malin's term, would single out the Talmud Torah as an "illuminating" demonstration of the importance of educational collaboration and consolidation:

There is a need for *consolidation of religious schools to create regional Jewish educational centers independent of synagogue control.* Such a measure would

free schools of the constraints imposed by the politics, finances, and other pressures of synagogue affairs. Clearly, the synagogues and local Jewish federation
would need to finance such a program. The success of such a program, the
Talmud Torah in St. Paul, is highly illuminating.[76]

Dashefsky and Shapiro's praise for St. Paul's move to establish a communal educational agency evoked something of Horace Mann's "common
school," along with the enduring influence of early-twentieth-century American Jewish educational theorists who had posited a dynamic relationship
between a self-aware "Jewish public" and its schools. Thinkers in this line
saw the cultivation of an inclusive, community-based outlook as a precondi-
tion for the continued development of Jewish life in an American context.
Some forty years earlier Barnett Brickner, also an early member of Benderly
and Kaplan's circle of educators, drew a direct analogy between public education, public health, and Jewish education, concluding:

Important as the function of the synagogue may be, the foundation of Jewish
unity is not the synagogue but the Jewish community, in whose membership will
be counted all Jews who are concerned with enriching Jewish life, in whatever
creative way, irrespective of whether they belong to the synagogue or not. . . .

Frankly, what is required is that you have the courage not to only formulate
but promulgate such a philosophy and insist that it should become the basis on
which a system of Jewish communal schools can be developed, and through
which the Jewish community of the future can be established. When this community has been established, then the synagogue will not be called upon to be
responsible for the Jewish school, because the Jewish community of which the
synagogue is an integral part, will become responsible for it.[77]

In singling out the Talmud Torah of St. Paul as an illuminating example of
the type of relationship between school, *shul*, and community Brickner had
advocated decades earlier, Dashefsky and Shapiro were affirming a vision
of Jewish community that by the 1970s had come to be associated with the
increasingly common expression "*clal Yisrael/collective Israel*." Though it
had an antique ring to it, the now widely used term, along with Kaplan's corresponding "Jewish peoplehood," was in fact of recent coinage, both expressions intended to convey this sense of broad and inclusive Jewish identity.[78]
The "Talmud Torah," in St. Paul and numerous other communities, though
not the public school that Mann envisioned, conveyed a similar sensibility. The broadened reconfiguration of the term "Talmud Torah" as a name
for such schools, having often been used in Europe for community-funded
schools for poorer children, resembled a similar transformation of the "common" in "common school." Beyond the Fund and Council's desire to promote
"efficiency and economy of administration," the origins and development of

the Talmud Torah reflected this inclusive, communal self-image—both the medium and the message of a vibrant sense of a "public self." Dashefsky, Shapiro, and Elazar, in drawing attention to St. Paul, weren't offering a blanket endorsement of the agency per se, with all of its shortcomings, but of the relationship between the community and its communal school.

This process accelerated with the appointment of Rabbi Joel (Yosi) Gordon as executive director in 1978, the fourth "Gordon" to play a pivotal role in Jewish education in the Twin Cities.[79] Though he had most recently served as the assistant director of Los Angeles Hebrew High School, Gordon grew up in Green Bay Wisconsin, received his BA from the University of Wisconsin, Madison, and had been a camper and longtime staff member at Camp Ramah, Wisconsin. The Midwestern-progressive-traditional, Hebrew-and-*Tanakh*-centered synthesis of the Twin Cities' Talmud Torahs resonated with his own educational background. Drawing on an array of friends and acquaintances in the area, reaching back to his years at Ramah, Gordon quickly acclimated himself to his new surroundings and set to work further advancing that curricular synthesis, along with the school's profile in the community.

Gordon initially focused his efforts on augmenting the faculty's teaching skills and Jewish learning, while significantly strengthening the Hebrew and textual facets of the curriculum. New Hebrew language, Hebrew Bible, and project-based curriculum materials that Gordon had helped to develop in Los Angeles were introduced into the Talmud Torah curriculum. In the spirit of the Dashefsky and Shapiro, Himmelfarb, and Bock studies, Gordon emphasized the teenage years as the "heart" of the school, pointing the curriculum toward academic opportunities that accrued with continued enrollment, to counter the common Jewish teenage impression of being on the descending side of a curricular peak.[80] Within a few years of his arrival, *midrashah* (high school) students were studying Tanakh in Hebrew, G'mara in Aramaic, and primary medieval and modern philosophical texts—along with contemporary Hebrew literature, studio arts, and popular Israeli music. The basement of the school would soon feature a *moadon*, replete with Hebrew language games and learning devices.

Gordon's tenure as director would be marked by an impressive series of achievements. In 1988, looking back on his first ten years in St. Paul, he would echo Dashefsky and Shapiro's observations regarding the distinctive virtues of the St. Paul community that made these successes possible:

> When synagogues throughout the country opened their own Hebrew schools to exert better control over content, to train B'nai Mitzvah and to provide a new service to their membership, the Talmud Torah of St. Paul was almost unscathed. The reasons are lost in history.

Maybe it was the example of the Minneapolis Talmud Torah which dominated all of Jewish life in our twin city for many years. Maybe it was the leadership of a few people who were dedicated to the concept of community education. Maybe it had something to do with the history of the UJFC, which has been almost unique among federations in its commitment to communal education.

The result is a very different kind of Jewish educational institution.[81]

By the mid-1980s, the fruits of thirty years of educational cooperation and professionalization were ready for the harvest.[82]

NOTES

1. The earliest Jewish settlers in the area benefited from the relatively high degree of comfort with intergroup contact and collaboration characteristic of the period. See W. Gunter Plaut, *The Jews in Minnesota, the First Seventy-five Years* (New York: American Jewish Historical Society, 1959), 8–48, and William D. Green, *A Peculiar Imbalance* (St. Paul: Minnesota Historical Society, 2007).

2. See Mary Lethert Wingerd, *Claiming the City: Politics, Faith, and the Power of Place in St. Paul* (Ithaca, NY: Cornell University Press, 2001), 37–39. McWilliams introduced his oft-cited characterization of Minneapolis in 1946 as "the capital of Anti-Semitism in the United States" by noting that anti-Semitism was "much more pronounced in Minneapolis than in St. Paul." McWilliams, too, would associate this divergence with the cities' respective social and ethnic characteristics. See Carey McWilliams, "Minneapolis: The Curious Twin," *Common Ground* (Autumn 1946): 61–66.

3. Harry Blackmun authored the 1973 Supreme Court *Roe v. Wade* decision. The chief justice at the time of the decision, Warren Burger, was also from St. Paul. The author heard Chuck McDew, a founder of the civil rights organization Student Nonviolent Coordinating Committee (SNCC), remark that after his most active years in the movement he moved to St. Paul because he was fascinated by the exceptionally high number of prominent African Americans who came from the city—adding that he specifically meant St. Paul, not Minneapolis.

4. http://usatoday30.usatoday.com/news/nation/2004-04-11-most-livable_x.htm.

5. W. Gunther Plaut, "A Hebrew-Dakota Dictionary," *Publications of the American Jewish Historical Society*, 42, no. 4 (June 1953): 361–70.

6. Plaut, *The Jews in Minnesota*, 30–35.

7. Most notably, through the precipitous growth of the Pillsbury and Washburn-Crosby milling companies, the latter company forming the core of what would become the General Mills Corporation.

8. Elizabeth Ann Lorenz-Meyer, *Gender, Ethnicity and Space: Jews in Minneapolis and St. Paul, 1900–1930* (Ann Arbor: ProQuest/UMI, 2006), 39. Lorenz-Meyer

notes a wide discrepancy in estimates of the Jewish population of Minneapolis in 1900 and settles on a rough mean, approximately equal to the Jewish population of St. Paul at the time, but by 1910 the Jewish population of Minneapolis appears to have been the larger of the two. Samuel Deinard, author of the entry on "Minnesota" in the Jewish Encyclopedia (1904), placed the Minneapolis Jewish population at 6000 and the St. Paul population at 5000.

9. Dashefsky and Shapiro, *Ethnic Identification among American Jews*, 18.

10. Virginia Brainard Kunz, *Saint Paul—The First 150 Years* (St. Paul: Saint Paul Foundation, 1991).

11. In is unclear when the first of these schools was officially established in St. Paul. See W. Gunther Plaut, *Mount Zion: 1856–1956* (St. Paul: North Central Publishing, 1956), 35. On the origins and decline of communal supplementary afternoon schools, see Stuart Kelman, ed., *What We Know about Jewish Education* (Los Angeles: Torah Aura, 1992), chapters 3, 17. See also, Louis Finkelstein, ed., *The Jews: Their History, Culture, and Religion* (Philadelphia: JPS, 1949), 924–33.

12. The synagogue, though founded by traditionally observant Jews, affiliated with the Reform Movement in 1878.

13. The circumlocution "Capital City" was no doubt intended to avoid the awkward conflation of "Hebrew School" with "St. Paul." In 1912 the school moved to it its own building on College Avenue, after having been housed by the Sons of Jacob and Sons of Abraham congregations. The building literally sat in the shadow of St. Paul, downhill from massive sculptures of Paul and Peter set above the front entry of the Cathedral of St. Paul.

14. M. Chiat and C. Proshan, *We Rolled Up Our Sleeves* (St. Paul: United Jewish Fund and Council of St. Paul, 1985), 77–78. Eleven years earlier, one estimate put the percentage of Jewish children in St. Paul receiving a "Hebrew Education" at 15 percent. See "Temple of Aaron: A Synagogue History," http://templeofaaron.org/media/Temple-of-Aaron-A-Synagogue-History.pdf. During the same period, comparably low percentages were observed in other locales around the country, including large Jewish population centers. However, the distinction between "not receiving" and "never attended" was potentially quite significant. So, for example, it was estimated in 1935, the same year as the St. Paul study, that only 25 percent of Jewish children in New York were receiving any form of Jewish education, though roughly 70 percent had received some formal Jewish education at some point in their lives. See: Nathan Glazer, *American Judaism* (Chicago: University of Chicago Press, 1957), 86. Cf. Jonathan B. Krasner, *The Benderly Boys and American Jewish Education* (Waltham, MA: Brandeis University Press, 2011), 41, 94, 334.

15. Louis Ginzberg, *Students, Scholars and Saints* (Philadelphia: JPS, 1928), 33–34.

16. Plaut, *The Jews of Minnesota*, 294.

17. Chiat and Proshan, *We Rolled Up Our Sleeves*, 76.

18. In addition to alleviating internal administrative tensions, this division would also qualify the recreational division to receive Community Chest funding. Chiat and Proshan, *We Rolled Up Our Sleeves*, 77.

19. The Center school in its various iterations was closely associated with the Temple of Aaron. The Jewish Educational Center and Hebrew School was located adjacent to the Temple of Aaron, near the intersection of Holly Avenue and Grotto Street. The Capital City and Center high school programs merged in 1933, followed by the elementary programs in 1944.

20. United Jewish Fund and Council Oral History Project, Kalman (Kokie) Goldenberg interview, August 29, 1983, http://reflections.mndigital.org/cdm/compound object/collection/jhs/id/836/rec/152.

21. United Jewish Fund and Council Oral History Project, Irwine Gordon interview, October 10, 1982, http://reflections.mndigital.org/cdm/ref/collection/jhs/id/890.

22. "St. Paul Unifies Jewish Education," *American Jewish World*, May 28, 1948, 1.

23. "St. Paul Hebrew Schools Merge," *American Jewish World*, June 4, 1948, 18.

24. Chiat and Proshan, *We Rolled Up Our Sleeves*, 79. Regarding the continued use of Yiddish at the Hebrew Institute, see YouTube interview with Linda Mack Schloff, January 20, 2012, https://www.youtube.com/watch?v=m8Rn734i6Gs.

25. Plaut, *The Jews of Minnesota*, 174–75. Mt. Zion's Religious School also remained, but it involved many fewer hours of instruction than the other supplementary programs.

26. The "Hebrew-in-Hebrew" (*ivrit-b'ivrit*) method entailed instruction in Hebrew with little or no recourse to a second language. The European *heder m'tukan* movement pioneered the development of the methodology. It would share other broader characteristics with initiatives in the United States associated with Benderly and Kaplan as well. On Benderly and his influence on Jewish education in the twentieth century, see Krasner's, *The Benderly Boys and American Jewish Education*.

27. On the *heder m'tukan* movement, see Finkelstein, *The Jews*, 927ff, and Benjamin Harshav, *Language in Time of Revolution* (Berkeley: University of California Press, 1993), 110. On the *heder m'tukan* movement in Lithuania, the birthplace of several of Minnesota's most influential twentieth-century Jewish educators, see Yisrael Klausner, *Vilna, Jerusalem of Lithuania* (Bnei Brak: Kibbutz ha-Meuhad, 1983), 588–89.

28. In the late 1960s, fifty years after Philip Kleinman's arrival in St. Paul, an elderly Samuel Baker, Kleinman's contemporary and one of the first graduates of the Teachers Institute at the Jewish Theological Seminary, joined the staff of B'nai Abraham Congregation in Minneapolis. Baker was the "last of the first" of Benderly's and Kaplan's students and protégés to make their way to the Twin Cities. In the intervening years, many others would leave their mark on Jewish education in Minneapolis and St. Paul.

29. Regarding the New York "Kehillah," see Krasner, *The Benderly Boys*, 39ff. Krasner's description of the founding of the Central Jewish Institute (CJI) in Manhattan, the "first modern Jewish educational center in the United States," established in 1916 and located next to Kehillath Jeshurun Synagogue, parallels developments in St. Paul in the years that followed. Along with the adoption of progressive educational techniques, including the *ivrit-b'ivrit* method, the St. Paul Jewish Educational Center, also located next to a traditional-progressive congregation, was nevertheless

conceived of as an independent communal institution with a combined educational, social, cultural, and recreational mission for all members of the community. On the Central Jewish Institute see Krasner, chapter 9. Regarding related developments in Christian settings, see David Kaufman, *Shul With a Pool: The Synagogue Center in American History* (Waltham, MA: Brandeis University Press, 1999), 4–5.

30. Rabbi Kleinman would move on to positions in Milwaukee and Portland, Oregon, while Anna Kleinman Schwartz continued her educational vocation. In her sixties she remained a memorable educator, teaching American history teacher at Lincoln Junior High School in North Minneapolis. Following her retirement from the Minneapolis school system, she taught at the Minneapolis Talmud Torah and served as librarian at the Minneapolis Jewish Community Center.

31. "Unified Education for St. Paul," *American Jewish World*, January 16, 1948, 8.

32. Chiat and Proshan, *We Rolled Up Our Sleeves*, 80.

33. Lorraine E. Pierce, "The Jewish Settlement on St. Paul's Lower West Side," *American Jewish Archives*, 28, no. 2 (November 1976): 143–61. Estimated 1948 Jewish population of St. Paul taken from http://www.jewishdatabank.org/Studies/downloadFile.cfm?FileID=2963.

34. Chiat and Proshan, *We Rolled Up Our Sleeves*, 79–80.

35. Kaplan is said to have paid the salaries of Hebrew Institute instructors form his own funds during the depression years (Interview with Harold Smith, May 22, 2015).

36. The new home of the Sholom Residence, renamed the George Kaplan Sholom Residence, would be built at the Randolph and Macalester site instead, opening in 1958. The Sholom Residence was founded by the daughters of Abraham Auxiliary of the Sons of Abraham Synagogue as a facility for the chronically ill. At the time, the Jewish Home for the Aged, also located in St. Paul, would only accepted healthy elderly residents. See Linda Mack Schloff, *And Prairie Dogs Weren't Kosher* (St. Paul: Minnesota Historical Society Press, 1996), 194, 209.

37. Among papers of Harry Rosenthal entrusted to Rachel Levitt. The author sincerely appreciates Rachel Levitt making this and other documents available to him.

38. United Jewish Fund and Council Oral History Project, Kalman (Kokie) Goldenberg interview, August 29, 1983.

39. Chiat and Proshan, *We Rolled Up Our Sleeves*, 79. At the time, Mt. Zion's one-day-a-week religious school had approximately 400 students. See http://mzion.org/wp-content/uploads/2011/03/Historical-Tidbits.pdf, 10. In his autobiography, Gunther Plaut, senior rabbi of Mt. Zion from 1948 to 1961, stressed the high degree of integration already characteristic of the St. Paul community upon his arrival, between "old and new, between the East and West European segments." See W. Gunther Plaut, *Unfinished Business* (Toronto: Lester & Orpen Dennys, 1981), 163–65.

40. "St. Paul Orthodox Hebrew Institute Asks Public Support," *American Jewish World*, January 13, 1956, 1. Morris C. Katz, "St. Paul Hebrew School Dispute," *American Jewish World*, March 16, 1956, 8. The irony that the Hebrew Institute was no more neutrally positioned, having moved in the summer of 1955 from the West Side to the Orthodox-affiliated Sons of Jacob Building on Portland Avenue, was, no doubt, not lost upon the supporters of the Mississippi River Boulevard plan.

41. Chiat and Proshan, *We Rolled Up Our Sleeves*, 79.

42. Katz, *American Jewish World*, March 16, 1956.

43. At this time, the Conservative movement was calling for a minimum of six hours a week of Jewish instruction. On Conservative educational standards in the 1950s, see Louis L. Ruffman, *Survey of Jewish Education in Minneapolis* (New York: AAJE, 1957), 41.

44. Ibid., 14. Mt. Zion's new building on Summit Avenue was dedicated in 1954. The Sons of Jacob building at 1466 Portland Avenue was completed in 1953. The Temple of Aaron's building was dedicated in 1956, a week before dedication ceremonies for the adjacent Talmud Torah building. Katz's misgivings regarding a shortened school week would eventually be born out.

45. Morris C. Katz, "What Are Really The Facts?" *American Jewish World*, February 24, 1956, 18.

46. *American Jewish World*, January 13, 1956, 1.

47. Linda M. Schloff, ed., "Who Knew? Stories Unearthed from the Archives," *Journal of the Jewish Historical Society of the Upper Midwest* (Fall 2011): 81.

48. The arrangement in St. Paul lasted for only a few years in the early 1930s. See Chiat and Proshan, *We Rolled Up Our Sleeves*, 76–77.

49. Daniel J. Elazar, "The Future of Central Agencies for Jewish Education," *Journal of Jewish Education*, 58, nos. 3–4 (Fall–Winter 1990): 8–10.

50. For Daniel J. Elazar's analysis of characteristics of the community that led to this status, see Elazar, *Community and Polity: The Organizational Dynamics of American Jewry* (Philadelphia: JPS, 1995), 353–54.

51. Lloyd P. Gartner, *Jewish Education in the United States, A Documentary History* (New York: Teachers College, 1969), 163.

52. Kaufman, *Shul with a Pool*, 146–47.

53. George Gordon's devotion to the community, as both a physician and an educator, was legendary. In an unfinished autobiographical account, Dr. Samuel Schwartz related that his mother, Ida Schwartz, had told him that after making a house call to treat a member of their impoverished family, Gordon would leave sufficient money with the prescription he had just written to pay for the medicine. Samuel Schwartz, *Legacies from Jewett Place, and Other Memoirs* (1996), chapter 1, 10–11.

54. Ruffman, *Survey of Jewish Education in Minneapolis*, 55–56.

55. Torah Academy was established in 1944 by families who considered the Minneapolis Talmud Torah curriculum inadequate and not sufficiently traditional. In the years immediately following Torah Academy's founding, the *American Jewish World* hosted a rancorous debate over the appropriateness of providing communal funds for Jewish "parochial" education. Nevertheless, in his 1957 study of Jewish education in Minneapolis, while commenting on the high proportion of girls attending the Talmud Torah (40 percent), Louis Ruffin also noted that the Conservative and Orthodox congregations either discouraged or did not allow boys to continue in their synagogue-based programs when they were of age to enter the Talmud Torah, encouraging enrollment in the Talmud Torah instead. Though a sexist artifact of the era, the practice indicates the degree to which high regard for the school was shared by Orthodox-affiliated community members as well. See Ruffman, *Survey of Jewish Education in Minneapolis*, 11. Significantly, Rabbi Moshe Feller, the first Chabad

shaliah to the Twin Cities, attended the Talmud Torah of Minneapolis until leaving the city to attend yeshivah. Indicative of subsequent changes among Orthodox-affiliated households were two efforts in the 1980s and 1990s to establish a progressive, modern orthodox-leaning high school in Minneapolis. Both efforts were short-lived, while an orthodox yeshiva and girl's school proved more durable.

56. In "The National-Cultural Movement in Hebrew Education in the Mississippi Valley" Elazar observes that as long as Louis Gordon was working in Superior, its Jewish education program was stronger that what was available in the larger Jewish community in Duluth, on the adjacent shore of Lake Superior.

57. L. Honor and E. Picheny, *Social, Recreational, and Educational Survey of the Jewish Community of Duluth* (Duluth, MN: Jewish Welfare Federation of Duluth, 1944), 37.

58. Ibid., 45.

59. Jacob R. Marcus, *United States Jewry, 1776–1985* (Detroit: Wayne State Press, 1993), 589.

60. Gartner, *Jewish Education in the United States*, 31. Harold Himmelfarb also noted that in the 1960s demographic studies indicated that a larger proportion of eligible children in smaller, as compared to larger, Jewish communities obtained "some Jewish schooling." Himmelfarb, "Jewish Education for Naught," 1.

61. L. I. Kaiser, "Minneapolis Is Different," *Jewish Education*, 50, no. 3 (Fall 1982): 34–38. Near the beginning of the article, Kaiser comments, "At regional meetings in Chicago, the נוסח was the same: 'Minneapolis is different,' but it would be wrapped in psukim of University of Chicago Sociology: 'Different social ecology, different social stratification, different culture[,] law, etc. . . . ; Let's skip it . . . let's hear from St. Paul or Milwaukee or Columbus."

62. Ibid., 37.

63. Plaut, *The Jews in Minnesota*, 174.

64. *American Jewish World*, January 13, 1956, 1.

65. "St. Paul Talmud Torah" and "Talmud Torah of St. Paul" would come to be used interchangeably, but as with the earlier circumlocution *"Capital City* Hebrew School," Talmud Torah *of St. Paul"* also may have initially struck some as incongruous.

66. The Hebrew-lettered cornerstone of a building on Logan Avenue in North Minneapolis that housed both a supplementary program and, for a time, the Torah Academy Day School, identifies the location as "Talmud Torah," though the date, 1937, was long after the establishment of the Talmud Torah of Minneapolis at another location. Similarly, the 1948 graduation program of the Center-Capital Hebrew School employs the title *Talmud Torah Merkaz* (*"Talmud Torah* Center"), "Talmud Torah" apparently referencing the "Capital City" portion of the title. Significantly, "Talmud Torah" doesn't appear anywhere, in Hebrew or English, in the 1951 BJE graduation booklet, or on BJE diplomas, which carried the legend *"Lishkat Hinuch Y'hudi,"* that is, Bureau of Jewish Education. Elazar also refers to the Center School as the "St. Paul Talmud Torah" in his "The National-Cultural Movement in Hebrew Education in the Mississippi Valley." Casual use of the term would lead many to view the new communal agency as simply a continuance of a preceding program. The

chapter on "Jews in Minnesota" in *They Chose Minnesota* (St. Paul: Minnesota Historical Society Press, 1981) repeats this misconception (497). This tendency is also reflected in a handwritten "Book of Graduates" passed down to the Talmud Torah that begins with the names of the 1923 graduates of the Temple of Aaron Hebrew School. Yearly lists of graduates follow, with no indication that the students were graduating from a series of different institutions—with one possible exception: a thick line extending a quarter of the way in from the left margin, between the fall class of 1956 and the spring class of 1957. Nevertheless, the fall class ends with graduate number 588, and the spring class picks up with graduate 589. On the use of the term "Talmud Torah" to describe communal schools in Europe and the United States, see: Finkelstein, *The Jews*, 924–30.

67. The name "St. Paul Talmud Torah/Talmud Torah of St. Paul" was inaugurated in conjunction with the opening of the Mississippi River Boulevard facility, a January 13, 1956 *American Jewish World* article (p. 1) noting that the Bureau of Jewish Education was "soon to be called the St. Paul Talmud Torah." However, the Talmud Torah's own list of presidents begins in 1949 with Arthur Bendel, shortly after the founding of the St. Paul Bureau of Jewish Education and the merger of its initial constituent programs.

68. Gedalia Leib (i.e., George Kaplan) Congregation, founded in 1955, was successor to two failing orthodox congregations. It closed in 1973, many of its remaining members moving to Sons of Jacob Congregation.

69. *American Jewish World*, June 22, 1956, 14.

70. Kaplan was a Jewish Theological Seminary (JTS) faculty member and the first director of the seminary's Teachers Institute. In March 1922, Kaplan's daughter Judith, who would marry Eisenstein, celebrated becoming a *bat mitzvah* by receiving the *maftir aliyah* and reciting the accompanying *haftarah*, the first recorded instance of such an occasion. Kaplan would have a profound influence on his student Bernard Raskas, who would serve as Senior Rabbi of the Temple of Aaron from 1953 to 1989.

71. Interview with Marvin Pertzik, June 25, 2015. Kokie Goldenberg recalled a similar comment by the same community member having been made during a solicitation visit he and Goldenberg made to a reluctant contributor. See United Jewish Fund and Council Oral History Project, Kalman (Kokie) Goldenberg interview, August 29, 1983.

72. Arnold Dashefsky and Howard M. Shapiro, "The Jewish Community of St. Paul" (1971), http://www.jewishdatabank.org/studies/downloadFile.cfm?FileID=2400.

73. Harold Smith, president of the Talmud Torah from 1967 to 1970, presents his perspective on these changes in *My Life: The First 95 Years* (St. Paul, MN: Celebrations of Life, 2014), 103.

74. Malin was coeditor, with Rabbi Harry Nelson, of the widely used *Model Seder* (Middle Village: Jonathan David, 1957; revised 1974), a *hagadah* intended for the use of "the children of Hebrew Schools" (p. 3), that is, supplementary schools.

75. Abraham P. Gannes, Gene Greenzweig, and George Pollak, *A Study of Jewish Education in St. Paul, Minnesota, 1977–1978* (New York: American Association for Jewish Education, 1978).

76. Dashefsky and Shapiro, *Ethnic Identification among American Jews*, 124.

77. Barnett Brickner, "Communal Responsibility of the Synagogue to the Jewish School," *Journal of Jewish Education*, 3, no. 3 (1931): 147, 151.

78. Krasner, *The Benderly Boys*, 325. Solomon Schecter's term "Catholic Israel" stems from a similar construction of Jewish identity.

79. Also George Gordon, Louis Gordon, and Irwine Gordon, a St. Paul lawyer and communal leader who was influential in establishing the Talmud Torah and was president of the agency at the time the facility on Mississippi River Boulevard was constructed.

80. For example, older students were eligible to participate in a weekly shabbat afternoon study group and *tikkunei leil Shavuot* hosted by Gordon.

81. Joel (Yosi) Gordon, "The Talmud Torah of St. Paul: A Picture of a Community School," *Pedagogic Reporter*, 34 (January 1988): 17.

82. On continued discussion of the plusses and minuses of educational consolidation in this period, see Leon. H. Spotts, "The Theory and Practice of Agency Mergers—with Special Reference to Jewish Education," *Journal of Jewish Communal Service*, 55, no. 3 (March 1979).

Chapter 2

The Last Quarter of the
Twentieth Century

They who sow in tears, shall reap in joy.

—Nellie Greenberg, quoting Psalm 126 at the laying of the
cornerstone of the George Kaplan Educational Building, June 17, 1956

In the last quarter of the twentieth century, the St. Paul Talmud Torah would
repeatedly demonstrate the virtues of a central educational agency, as it
focused and circulated the community's educational energies.

Beginning in the late 1970s the Talmud Torah initiated a number of collaborative projects with other communal organizations and programs. At
the time, enrollments, though lower than the combined enrollment of the
Hebrew Institute and Bureau schools in the mid-fifties, and lower than its own
enrollment in the sixties, remained at well over 300 students.[1] A large early
childhood education program drew children from across the community,
well-attended adult classes were offered, and after-school suburban satellite
branches were formed. Cooperative Hebrew language and liturgical literacy
programs with the Temple of Aaron and Mount Zion Congregation were
instituted, and the Chabad/Lubavitch community used the Talmud Torah
building for summer youth programming. A joint adult education program
with the Jewish Community Center was established, a Talmud Torah Young
Judea chapter was started, a faculty study group was formed, and a collaborative communal workers education program, held at the St. Paul Jewish Community Center and led by a Talmud Torah faculty member, was launched.

The school also initiated major curriculum projects in Hebrew language
instruction and moral education. The latter project began in 1979 with a comment by Harry Rosenthal to a group of Talmud Torah teachers at the conclusion of a teacher-training seminar he had funded. Rosenthal, who had chaired

the committee that oversaw construction of the Kaplan Education Building twenty-three years earlier, told the group that he had been deeply troubled to discover that a graduate of the school had stolen from his business. As a result, he announced, he would be willing to fund the implementation of an ethics curriculum at the school. Gordon followed up on Rosenthal's offer, resulting in a moral education curriculum project that would have a significant impact on the character of the school for years to come.[2]

In addition to its moral development component, the school's curriculum would be firmly anchored in Hebrew language learning, classical Jewish texts, Jewish practice, and the arts. To teach these subjects, Gordon continued to build on the accomplished group of educators Malin had assembled. Faculty members were encouraged to attend conferences and teacher enrichment programs in the United Sates and Israel, with financial assistance provided. The staff included experts in a wide range of fields, and in two cases, family members of renowned Jewish educators. In the late 1970s faculty members Aya Schlair, daughter of Israel Prize recipient Siegfried Lehmann and founder of the Ben Shemen Youth Village, and Joe Honor, grandson of Leo Honor, the highly accomplished student of Samson Benderly and coauthor of the 1944 study of Jewish education in Duluth, taught across the hall from one another. Talmud Torah administrators and faculty members from this period would include six authors of books related to Jewish life and learning.[3]

These developments coincided with a rapid rise in the number of nonorthodox Jewish day schools across the country. In 1982, the Talmud Torah also added a day school to its programs, two years before an independent day school, initially housed in the Talmud Torah of Minneapolis facility, was formed across the river. The AAJE report that accompanied Harry Malin's departure had encouraged consideration of a day school for the community, leading to inconclusive discussions with Torah Academy, the Orthodox-affiliated school in Minneapolis, about establishing a St. Paul branch.[4] The founding, instead, of a communal day school four years later, under the aegis of the Talmud Torah, bespoke a burgeoning confidence in the community's educational agency. Ruth Gavish had joined the Talmud Torah administrative staff in 1980 as principal of the afternoon school, but directing a day school had also figured in planning for her position, and in 1982 she became the first principal of the Talmud Torah of St. Paul Day School.

Day School enrollment grew from 21 to 103 students in its first four years,[5] and by the mid-1990s approached 200 students. The school's first three principals, Ruth Gavish, Susan Cobin, and Cindy Reich, would build on the curricular strengths of the supplementary program, while taking advantage of the full-day schedule to develop a highly innovative, integrated Jewish studies—general studies curriculum. Along with strong science, math, language arts, fine arts (choir, dance, visual arts), and social studies instruction, the curriculum would also emphasize classical Jewish texts, the Hebrew language, halakhic competencies, civic engagement, and the development of moral judgment. In the Day School, the Rosenthal curriculum project would lead to a pioneering "school justice committee"/"*Va'ad Din*" program, which was integrated with the fifth- and sixth-grade Tanakh and Mishnah curricula. Informed by Harvard psychologist Lawrence Kohlberg's work in moral development, and inspired by Janusz Korczak's educational methods, the *Vaad Din* provided students the opportunity to exercise genuine authority in the resolution of school-related disputes and policy questions, that they might learn from both the decision-making process and the resulting responsibilities they bore for their decisions. The Justice Committee initiative was, in turn, the basis of an "Intercommunal Justice Committee Network," run in cooperation with the Minneapolis Jewish Day School, the Taylors Falls School District (approximately 50 miles north of St. Paul), Trinity Catholic school (St. Paul), and Tuttle School, a public school in Southeast Minneapolis. Many of the memorable guests who came to the Talmud Torah in this period to speak with students did so in connection with this aspect of the curriculum.

The cultures and curricula of the agency's schools were deeply enriched by the diverse social backgrounds of students, faculty members, and administrators, while the Jewish and general communities were beneficiaries of the relationships nurtured under its auspices. Many students came from "old" St. Paul families, or were otherwise well-connected to the Jewish community, but a significant number of students were from unaffiliated families. In the 1980s and 1990s, the St. Paul Jewish community resettled a disproportionally large number of households from the Soviet Union and Eastern Europe, as compared with other Jewish communities across the country. Communal agencies cooperated in connecting the children of these families with the Talmud Torah and providing the financial support necessary to make its programs affordable. These children significantly augmented Day School enrollment in particular, while broadening its social and cultural base. The schools also included faculty members and students from other locales and Jewish cultures (Yemenite, Georgian, Bulgarian, Persian-Iranian). While helping to broaden awareness of intra-Jewish diversity, these students, staff members, and their families often found involvement in a communal school more personally consequential than membership in a synagogue.

During this period, doubts about the quality and safety of St. Paul's public schools, along with little affinity among Jews for the private alternatives then available, undoubtedly contributed to the Day School's appeal. The Talmud Torah's schools also benefited from strong personal and institutional ties to the St. Paul Fund and Council, the St. Paul Jewish Community Center, the local Hillel Foundation, the St. Paul Jewish Family Service, and congregations throughout the Twin Cities. The resulting network of relationships formed among students and faculty confirmed the Talmud Torah's value as a social and educational meeting place for Jews of differing orientations and affiliations, and a vital link to the larger community. Along with hundreds of active, Jewishly informed community members, alumni from the last third of the century would include numerous rabbis, academics, Jewish educators and education program directors, university award-winning Hebrew and Jewish studies graduates, staff members of a wide array of Jewish advocacy and social service organizations, community agency and organization directors, the president of a national Jewish philanthropic foundation, national Jewish periodical editors and journalists, a member of the Board of Visitors of the Mosse/Weinstein Center for Jewish Studies, a Caro Geniza research specialist, and a biblical novelist who attributed the basis of her technique to what she had learned about *midrash* at the school.

By the mid-1980s, much of the Jewish educational impetus in the Twin Cities had shifted from Minneapolis and its larger agencies to their counterparts in St. Paul, where a smaller population appeared an asset when it came to institutional agility and inclusion.[6] Articles about Talmud Torah initiatives appeared in numerous anthologies and periodicals, including *The Jewish Teacher's Handbook* (Vol. III), *What We Know About Jewish Education*, *The Pedagogic Reporter* (JESNA), *Journal of Religious Education*, *Jewish Education News* (a publication of the Coalition for the Advancement of Jewish Education/CAJE), and the youth periodical *Baba Ganewz*.

A measure of the agency's growing prominence in this period is also evident from a list of visitors. Guests included Lawrence Kohlberg, who spent a morning in 1986 discussing the moral implications of a biblical passage with Day School fourth graders[7]; Israel Knesset member Col. Meir Pail, who spoke to a gathering of afternoon school students in the fall of 1979 about a "two-state solution" to the Israel-Palestinian conflict, and Israeli-Palestinian writer Anton Shammas, who discussed his work as a poet and journalist, along with dilemmas faced by Arab Israelis, with afternoon school students. Printmaker Mordecai Rosenstein reflected on his development as a visual artist with Day School students, educator and author Zvi Adar spoke with faculty about teaching Tanakh, and *Melitz* founder and director Avraham Infeld spoke with students and faculty about his work. Dr. Henry Smith, a highly respected nephrologist, spoke with afternoon school students about his term on a committee responsible for rationing life-saving access to kidney dialysis, when the procedure was still new and far too few machines were available. The former US army officer identified as "Lt. Wayne Marshall" in the United Synagogue book *When Life Is in the Balance*, spoke with a group of sixth-grade Day School students about his role in the incident described in the book,[8] and Jerusalem's *Yad LeKashish* (Workshop for the Aged) founder

Miriam Mendelow spoke with Day School students about her personal journey to a life of service. Afternoon school students met with National Jewish Book Award and Israel Prize recipient Natan Shaham. Hamline University Law School Dean and former St. Paul mayor George Latimer, Chief Kadi of Israel Ahmed Natur, and Hebrew University Law Professor Zev Falk spoke to Day School students in conjunction with their service on the *Va'ad Din/ School Justice Committee*,[9] and Minnesota Attorney General Skip Humphrey met with Day School students, along with students from three other schools in the Intercommunal Justice Committee Network, to talk about his work, and theirs.

That such prominent guests made their way to the St. Paul Talmud Torah is itself noteworthy, but the list also suggests the degree to which Talmud Torah curricula were at one and the same time deeply rooted in Jewish life, while focused on helping students to better understand and constructively engage the world around them.

The period wasn't without its rough spots. Some found Gordon overly assertive, the Day School curriculum too loose, the afternoon school too demanding. The Hebrew curriculum project did not produce a complete published curriculum, and in addition to the study that accompanied Harry Malin's departure, dissatisfaction among some parents would result in two more Jewish Education Service of North America (JESNA) reports.[10] And, despite sustained total enrollments, the numbers were low when measured against the community's total population, especially for teenagers, even when allowances were made for students in programs sponsored by Mt. Zion and Chabad. A 1993 study of the St. Paul community found that while sixty-two percent (62 percent) of the children in the pre-bar/bat mitzvah stage (aged 11–13) were enrolled in formal Jewish education programs, only 35 percent remained enrolled post bar/bat mitzvah age.[11]

Nevertheless, the overall trajectory of the agency was unmistakably upward. Academic expectations were rising and outcomes were impressive. Successful new programs and collaborations were leading to unmistakable benefits for the school and the community. The Talmud Torah was coming to be seen among Jews, and to a significant degree, beyond the Jewish community as well, as a distinguished asset and worthy expression of the aspirations of the St. Paul Jewish community. A small community, wrapped around a bend on the upper Mississippi, had built a school that was providing what many schools around the country, in larger and wealthier Jewish communities, dearly hoped to offer: a range of excellent early childhood, supplementary, adult, and day school programs with student bodies drawn from a wide spectrum of backgrounds and affiliations, offered under one roof, by a central communal agency; programs rooted in a classical Jewish curriculum, with a special focus on moral education, strong ties to the larger St. Paul community, and impressive academic outcomes, including an outstanding general studies program in the Day School.

HOW DID THIS HAPPEN?

At the St. Paul United Jewish Fund and Council's 1985 Annual Meeting, Fund Executive Director Kim Marsh drew his listeners' attention to educational developments in the community:

> We are shrinking, graying. . . . Despite this adversity, there are significant developments which I believe to be the harbingers of our future success: a significant increase in Jewish education both at the Talmud Torah in the Day School and in its wonderful Marjorie Smith Hoffman Learning Center. . . . Moreover, we're not Jewish chauvinists, and communally we recognize the need to support other day schools as well (such as the Lubavitch Cheder and Torah Academy). . . .
>
> How do we assure creative Jewish continuity? I believe that the linchpin is in the provision of quality Jewish education *for ourselves and for our children and grandchildren.*[12]

Marsh's vision was inspiring. The community was "shrinking and graying," but signs of renewed vitality in Jewish education were "harbingers of our future success." A thirty-year arc of educational growth and professionalization, sustained by the focused use of communal resources, was now yielding impressive results. Growing enrollments of students living in Minneapolis (and beyond) in St. Paul Talmud Torah programs,[13] in some cases leading to families moving to St. Paul, suggested that the effective coordination of the community's educational resources was already helping, in substantive ways, to stem the "shrinking and graying" of the community. It was a propitious moment, marked by the convergence of farsighted communal leaders, willing benefactors, and talented educators; a "confluence of people and factors," in the words of Harold Smith, an influential figure in the unfolding events.[14]

However, Marsh's comments must be located in a larger context, including the following factors:

1. St. Paul's longstanding pluralistic tendencies nurtured the Jewish community's civic aspirations. By the early 1960s, congregational rabbis Bernard Raskas and Gunter Plaut had both attained a significant public presence, Plaut purportedly going as far as to contemplate a run for city office.[15] That a rabbi would consider himself electable by an electorate that included relatively few Jews clearly reflects these tendencies. St. Paul would elect its first Jewish mayor in 1972 (followed by its first Lebanese-Irish mayor), but there were street-level indications of a

positive social environment as well. In the Highland Park neighborhood, home to the majority of St. Paul Jews from the 1960s through the 1980s, Ruben's Kosher Butcher shop and Cecil's Delicatessen were comfortably ensconced across the street from the College of St. Catherine, and a few blocks to the south a "Jewish holidays" panel graced the calendar mosaic that stretched across the exterior of Powers Department Store, built in 1960 at the neighborhood's central intersection. The chapter on the Twin Cities in *A Tale of Ten Cities*, a series of sketches of interreligious relations around the country, published in 1962 and coedited by St. Paul native Albert Vorspan, suggests a similar environment. The chapter's title, "St. Paul and Minneapolis—Unlike Twins," alludes to Carey McWilliams's "Minneapolis: The Curious Twin," and though ample evidence of persistent anti-Semitism in Minnesota is provided, when the authors turn to indications of "good will and understanding," all five examples include a connection to St. Paul.[16]

2. Through the middle decades of the century, though riven by socioeconomic and halakhic differences, nothing like the polarizing factions that had bedeviled East Coast advocates of communal education developed in St. Paul; no insular orthodox enclaves, detached Reform congregations, or an organized, doctrinaire hard-left presence in either St. Paul or Minneapolis. The relative absence of such forces left ample room for the liberal—socialist—labor Zionist orientation of Benderly inflected schools to take hold. Older Jews might still read the *Forvarts*, and there were Workman's Circle chapters in both communities, but little support for *Yiddishist* education. In the Jewish New York the Kleinmans left behind, Jewish anarchists and communists had taunted the observant with Yom Kippur dinners and dances, but storming the barricades of the shul down the street held little allure for Upper-Midwestern Jewish progressives.[17] Rather, the Jews of St. Paul constituted a relatively secure, well-integrated community, enveloped by the left-of-center social reform ethos of Wisconsin Progressives and Minnesota Farmer-Laborites.[18] The emergence of Chabad as a distinct presence in St. Paul would eventually modify the community's profile, but Daniel J. Elazar would attribute his father Albert Elazar's decision in 1929 to take a teaching position with one of the "Talmud Torahs" in St. Paul to characteristics that would persist through the end of the century:

> Almost immediately on his arrival in the United States, he found the immigrant Jewish ghettos of the East not to be for him and in general found the eastern United States to embody a way of life that was less attractive to him than the American Midwest and West. Within six months of his arrival in the United States he accepted a position in Minnesota and he moved himself from New York to St. Paul and Minneapolis. From then on until

he returned to Israel, his life was intertwined with that part of the country, roughly the Mississippi River Valley at its heart and at its broadest extent, and he identified with it fully, working to build Jewish life in those regions that were a synthesis of the two civilizations.

My father never lived elsewhere in the United States, although he was offered positions in other parts of the country. He found what he was seeking in the Mississippi Valley–Great Lakes watershed region, broadly understood. He had the open-ness, energy, and basic sense of trust that was characteristic of people from that interior part of the country. Among other aspects of Americanism, midwestern-style, he rapidly integrated into the Progressive spirit as it was expressed in that region, but always with common sense.[19]

3. Elazar would also suggest that a disproportionate number of Lithuanian Jews in the region had exerted a decisive influence in educational matters; Jews who, while devoted to traditional Jewish learning, brought with them a more urbane and progressive attitude toward the study of the Jewish past and construction of a Jewish future. Influential educational figures in the Twin Cities certainly fit this description. The surname "Gordon," shared by many of these figures, is a characteristically Lithuanian-Jewish name.[20]

4. Immigrants, including holocaust survivors, along with their first-generation American children, still exerted a strong influence on the community Marsh surveyed. The "graying" segments of the community were, by and large, these immigrant and first-generation Jews, who comprised both assimilationist and traditionalist tendencies. Though the Jewish children of St. Paul in the latter half of the twentieth century were largely American born and fully shaped by mainstream American culture (excepting new arrivals from the Soviet Union and Eastern European countries), they continued to live alongside older Jews who were not.

5. Though in the mid-1980s the American economy was emerging from a downturn, it had been preceded by decades of economic expansion. St. Paul's aging Jewish population included prosperous individuals who shared Marsh's perspective on the role Jewish education would play in the future of the community, and were prepared to invest in that future. Many of these benefactors had deep roots in St. Paul, owned brick-and-mortar businesses that reinforced their local roots, and were inclined to contribute to communal as well as congregational causes, leading to a dramatic surge of construction of both communal and synagogue buildings in the 1950s and 1960s.[21]

6. The dominant dynamic among young American Jews in the 1960s and 1970s remained assimilationist, but a secondary tendency was emerging that reaffirmed Jewish life as a counter-cultural response to the

disappointments and disarray of American life at the end of the 1960s. A morally acute engagement with traditional Jewish life offered an alternative to the inadequacies of both bland suburbia and drugs-sex-and-rock-and-roll. By the early 1970s the cautiously liberal tone of "A Gentleman's Agreement" had been superseded by the boldly assertive tenor of "Fiddler on the Roof," while Klezmer bands played to large and enthusiastic audiences. Chabad, deftly casting its strain of *hasidut* as a sound next step for disillusioned children of the 1960s, was meeting with considerable success.[22]

This surge of self-affirmation paralleled developments in other segments of American society, epitomized by the publication of Alex Haley's *Roots in* 1976, followed a year later by the television adaption, which reached an unprecedented one hundred thirty million viewers.[23] Reflecting these influences, Harold Himmelfarb framed his findings regarding a minimal number of instructional hours necessary to influence adult attitudes and behavior in terms of the "culturally deprived Jewish child," akin to, and yet distinct from the circumstances faced by "poor whites, blacks, Chicanos and other minority groups that are normally considered among the 'culturally deprived.'"[24] Alongside a surge in academic programs in African African-American, Native American, Chicano, and Asian studies, Jewish studies programs were established at colleges and universities around the country, including the University of Minnesota, and their graduates were in need of employment. These formal academic programs found their complement in a profusion of *havurot*, study groups, and adult education programs. Through the 1980s and 1990s, hundreds of St. Paul Jews, from all segments of the community, participated in such groups and programs, including a highly successful Melton Mini-School, hosted by the St. Paul Jewish Community Center.

7. Significant numbers of young Jews were visiting Israel, which was still commonly viewed in the afterglow of its Labor-Zionist origins and the traumatic drama of the Six Day and Yom Kippur wars. The revival of Hebrew as the spoken language of a large proportion of Jews signaled a turning point in Jewish history. Acquiring Hebrew language skills connected Jews not only to one another, but to the historical moment. Benjamin Harshav asserted that one could go so far as to say that the State of Israel resulted from "*an ideology that created a language that forged a society that became a state.*"[25] The role of the Hebrew language, Harshav contended, was pivotal to the process, and Jews around the world had resonated with the phenomenon. At the outset of this new era, Hillel Levine chastised attendees at the 1969 meetings of Council of Jewish Federations and Welfare Funds:

For some it was a trip to Israel, for others it was the reading of Buber's *I and Thou*, for others an encounter with Hasidism, for others it was a traditional Jewish education redirected to confront existential problems. . . . The Six Day War forced us to reassess our attachment in deciding to risk our lives if necessary on Israel's behalf. The black awakening reminded us that the melting pot dream was a fool's fantasy and that differences were legitimate. We woke up from the American dream and tried to discover who we really were. For many of us this now means turning our concerns inward into the Jewish community because we are disenchanted with the crass materialism of the larger society.

We know of the historical generative powers of Jewish education and its stimulation of a meaningful Jewish life. . . . But the possibilities of Jewish education cannot be seen simply in terms of keeping Jews within the folds or training future *machers*. Jewish education must compensate for the shortcomings of the educational system in character building and stimulating moral sensitivity. Living in more than one culture can give young Jews valuable perspective. Quality Jewish education will help the individual remain whole in a society which denies sanctity to the human vessel.[26]

8. Jewish summer camps were thriving in Minnesota and neighboring Wisconsin that complemented and supplemented Talmud Torah curricula while forging relationships among campers and staff. Camp Ramah in Wisconsin (Conservative), Olin Sang Ruby Union Institute (Reform), and Herzl Camp (independent), all founded between 1946 and 1952 and committed to extensive Jewish programming, drew large numbers of campers, staff, and benefactors from the Twin Cities.

9. Educational efforts in St. Paul enjoyed the backing of the community's congregational rabbis. The support of Bernard Raskas, Temple of Aaron's senior rabbi from 1951 to 1989 and a prominent communal leader, proved crucial in this regard. Many would come to see him as representative of a populist reaction against traditional Jewish practice and erudition, but Raskas was himself an academic standout at Jewish Theological Seminary, with a strong affinity for those who, like Mordecai Kaplan, stressed the development of broad-based communal institutions. He would collide on occasion with communal agency directors over questions of programmatic purview, but his support for the Talmud Torah would significantly boost the school's standing in the community. During his years at the Temple of Aaron, the largest of St. Paul's synagogues, elementary age children in the congregation were expected to attend the Talmud Torah, and older students were encouraged to continue.[27]

Support for greater educational emphasis on the Hebrew language and traditional Jewish sources would also come from Mt. Zion's rabbis, whose personal affinities for the Talmud Torah's curriculum presaged a reaffirmation of Hebrew and traditional practices in Reform circles nationally. Unlike in Minneapolis, where Reform-affiliated Temple Israel would lead the way in displacing the Talmud Torah from its central position in the community, Reform rabbis in St. Paul were largely supportive of the Talmud Torah and the direction its curriculum was taking. A significant number of children from Mt. Zion were enrolled in both a Talmud Torah program and one of the congregation's own educational programs during this period.[28]

10. Local students weren't left wondering if their home communities saw any value in pursuing Jewish studies beyond a rudimentary level, or how they might do so. At a time when a sizable portion of Minnesota's Jewish youth went on to attend the University of Minnesota, evolving iterations of Near Eastern Studies, Hebrew, and Jewish Studies programs at the University—clearly a point of pride among Twin Cities Jews—offered accessible next steps in Jewish learning.[29]

11. The first wave of younger teachers and administrators directly shaped by the foregoing factors were taking up positions in Jewish schools, congregations, and other communal institutions across the country. For these educators, traditional practice and classical texts, proficiency in Hebrew, and strong links to the State of Israel, constituted educational common ground. International Coalition for the Advancement of Jewish Education (CAJE) conferences were begun, strengthening a sense of Jewish educational renaissance among the hundreds of participants who met annually to share curricula and forge personal connections.[30]

The same year that Marsh spoke of his guarded optimism for the community, in a short essay appended to a history of the St. Paul United Jewish Fund and Council, Talmud Torah Executive Director Gordon laid out a confident agenda for the agency: Expanding the day school through the eighth grade; educationally integrating the early childhood program with the day school; further development of informal education programs, in cooperation with synagogues and other communal agencies, to enhance the scope and efficacy of the afternoon school; establishing stronger links with camping and Israel programs; establishing a pre-college counseling program to help prepare students to continue growing Jewishly while in college; offering a complete family education program for all departments of the agency; publication of the Hebrew curriculum under development, along with other curriculum projects; development of facilities and staff for these new initiatives; the development of Talmud Torah branches to serve families in more remote suburban areas—and, the cultivation of the "hope that our community will survive and flourish, led by committed and creative

Jews who have learned, and continue to learn, Torah; who are knowledgeable and at home in their tradition."[31]

A 1990 JESNA study of the agency confirmed Marsh's and Gordon's
optimism, characterizing both the Supplementary School and Day School as
"a very good school." It recommended that "the communal system should be
maintained," and encouraged the strengthening of its base in the community.
Regarding this latter concern, the report proposed a communal education
planning process under the direction of the UJFC, and that a communal
"Jewish Education Committee with broad powers to make macro decisions
regarding global Jewish educational issues" be established, along with a
consultative "Board of Rabbis" and independent "Principal's Council." Significantly, however, the report also referenced "communal perceptions" that
would become points of contention in the years to come, centering on "elitist"
attitudes, favoring of the Day School over the other programs, and narrowing
of the agency's communal mandate, leading to recommendations regarding the composition of the agency's Board and its relation to the school's
administration.[32]

In short, an integrated Jewish "public" was emerging in St. Paul, energized
by related developments in Jewish communities around the world, and the
Talmud Torah was a local catalyst and beneficiary of these developments.
Building on this momentum, it cofounded, with the Minneapolis Jewish
Day School, the Twin Cities Jewish Middle School (TCJMS) in 1996, and
a University of Minnesota "College in the Schools" Hebrew program soon
followed.

Something of the hub-and-spoke dynamic long sought by advocates of a
central Jewish educational agency was emerging, culminating with the acquisition of the old Edgcumbe School building on Hamline Avenue, two miles
to the east of the River Road facility, to serve as a new, larger home for the
agency. The Marjorie Smith Hofman Educational Building, the new address
of the Supplementary School, Day School, Early Childhood Education
Program, and Twin Cities Middle School, opened in 1997. Talmud Torah–
associated programs would form a significant portion of the public presence
of the St. Paul Jewish community in this period. Student performance groups
would represent the community at arts festivals and other events, and Middle
School students at state academic tournaments. An article on the Intercommunal Justice Committee Network would appear in the Minneapolis Star
Tribune,[33] on Jewish communal education in St. Paul and plans for opening
of the Middle School, in the St. Paul Pioneer Press,[34] on Minnesota Attorney
General Hubert (Skip) Humphrey's visit to the Day School in the American
Jewish World[35]—all indicative of a vibrant institution.

As the 1990s came to a close, the new facility was brimming with educational energy. Susan Cobin, former principal of the St. Paul Day School and

the Twin Cities Middle School, would recount a conversation with a stranger in Jerusalem sometime in the late 1990s. When Cobin indicated that she was from St. Paul the new acquaintance replied, "They have a great day school there!"[36]

These developments confirmed the prescience of consolidating programs and the fostering of a traditional curriculum, leavened by progressive educational methods and a liberal ethos. The progressive-traditional character of the city, and the smaller-but-not-too-small size of the Jewish community recommended such a course. Circumstance had bolstered foresight.[37] By contrast, Benderly's initial efforts in New York to devise a suitable and effective educational model for American Jewish youth were linked to the founding, and foundering, of New York's *Kehillah* initiative. The *Kehillah*, established in 1908, was conceived of by its founders as an American version of the integrated administrative structures of Eastern European Jewish communities, weaving all of Jewish New York into a single, democratically accountable organizational fabric, but it quickly proved no match for the divisions and dissension it faced, and was effectively dissolved in 1922. However, such a model *could* gain some traction in a city like St. Paul. St Paul was largely beyond the reach of heavy-handed interference by national Jewish organizations and institutions with headquarters and base constituencies in the Eastern states. In the 1930s, as communal educational bureaus and alliances across the country were succumbing to factionalism and increased financial responsibilities occasioned by the Depression, the Talmud Torah of Minneapolis continued to flourish. And immediately following World War II, when economic conditions remained difficult, the St. Paul community had also proven an exception, pressing ahead with plans for a community agency of its own. Publication in November 1946 of New York educator Judah Pilch's elegiac Jewish Education article "Is the Talmud Torah Doomed?" coincided with a quickening of efforts in St. Paul to establish a communal Talmud Torah, while across the river, the Talmud Torah of Minneapolis thrived. Several years earlier, with depression era retrenchment eating away at a generation of educational reforms, Isaac Berkson had lamented that "the idea of a community supported Jewish education has not taken real root. In a sense, Jewish education remains a parasitical plant,"[38] but in Minneapolis it *had* taken root, and in St. Paul it would.

A relatively cooperative local leadership, the community's demographic profile, and broader Jewish and American cultural trends had all contributed to the ensuing successes. While community schools were giving way to synagogue-based programs around the country, including in Minneapolis, the St. Paul Talmud Torah's programmatic growth and educational successes in the 1960s, 1970s, and 1980s demonstrated that it remained a well-suited match for the community's expectations, assets, and needs.[39] Success had come on the heels of geographic, socioeconomic, and ideological convergence among St. Paul's Jews. Momentary setbacks and personal disappointments with one or another of the agency's programs—a fire, student in-groups and out-groups, faculty shortcomings—though troubling, could not dampen the broader optimism.

And yet, divisions in the St. Paul Jewish community were also reemerging, in some cases associated with the very developments Marsh lauded. By the mid-1980s, residential patterns were once again becoming more diffuse, and new Conservative and Reform congregations were founded.[40] Talmud Torah faculty and families figured prominently in the founding of Beth Jacob Congregation, in particular.[41] Relationships and attitudes fostered in the Talmud Torah's schools would have a direct bearing on the new congregation's composition and character, formed through the merger of a much-shrunken Sons of Jacob Congregation, the home of anti-Talmud Torah dissidents in the 1950s, and the recently established "New Conservative Congregation."

Along with Talmud Torah–associated founders, several early leaders of Beth Jacob had previously participated in an "alternative minyan" at Temple of Aaron, which would complicate connections between the two Conservative-affiliated congregations. Initially housed at the St. Paul Jewish Community Center, the new congregation, its name the legacy of Sons of Jacob, relocated to a new building in Mendota Heights, not far from the old "West Side" of St. Paul. Members would take pride in the congregation's "traditional-egalitarian" character, influenced by the Talmud Torah ethos. In the years that followed, every nonorthodox rabbi in the community not employed by another congregation would be a member of Beth Jacob.[42]

However, some community members would come to see the new congregation as a manifestation of Day School–fueled elitism, where enrollments had reached 103 by 1987, while supplementary school enrollments had dipped to 175.[43] From animosity toward the Pharisees and their rabbinic successors, to fissures between *hasidim*, *mitnag'dim*, and *maskilim*, to the emergence of the Reform Movement and the ensuing precipitation of Orthodox reaction, comparative worthiness and competence has proven, time and again, a ready source of tension among Jews.[44] Even the Benderly circle, though explicitly committed to education by and for communities, hadn't been immune to such attitudes.[45] Differing attitudes regarding Beth Jacob would typify, on a local scale, this longstanding conundrum of effective Jewish education.

The purchase and expansion of the new Talmud Torah building on Hamline Avenue also did not meet with universal approval. Some saw the move as overreaching. Up until this point, it had not been unusual for Talmud Torah students to move easily between the Talmud Torah and Temple of Aaron buildings for various purposes, and in the early 1990s, the rapid growth of the Day School led to rental of space from the synagogue. The greater part of the Talmud Torah's combined student body would continue to be affiliated with the Temple of Aaron into the 1990s, but the move to Hamline Avenue was seen by many as yet another indication of a widening ideological and functional gap between the Temple of Aaron and its erstwhile neighbor.[46]

Resulting strains and resentments would soon converge on the Talmud Torah. Beginning in the mid-1990s, Temple of Aaron leadership pressed the agency to institute a one-day-week supplementary school option—a step Hebrew Institute advocate Morris Katz no doubt would have characterized as the dropping of the other shoe, some thirty years after the Talmud Torah ceded Sunday mornings to synagogue-based programming. Negotiations to retain the congregation's support of the supplementary program extended through the end of the 1990s, but ultimately proved fruitless, the Temple of Aaron opening its own supplementary program in 2000.[47]

In the wake of these developments, congregational cooperation in support of a communal educational agency for St. Paul was once again in doubt, now due, it seemed, at least in part, to the founding of a congregation whose roots led back to the Talmud Torah's own energizing influence.[48]

Mt. Zion's connections to the Talmud Torah would weaken as well. The congregation would eventually discontinue contracting with the Talmud Torah to provide the Hebrew language component of its own education program, and while Adath Israel-affiliated students had always been a relatively small proportion of the Talmud Torah's total student body, there would soon be none.

The agency continued to flourish as these changes were unfolding, but questions about its proper role in the community grew. Did the Day School render the supplementary program and its constituency "second best"? Could the Day School truly serve the broader interests of the community, given the expense it entailed? Was the Talmud Torah facilitating or undermining a productive balance between quality and diversity of educational options? Was the school, in fact, fostering renewed factionalism? By the end of the 1990s the "public" character of the school had been seriously undercut by such concerns.

NOTES

1. The supplementary school had 335 students in 1978, Yosi Gordon's first year as Executive Director. See Gordon, "The Talmud Torah of St. Paul," 20. From 1962 to 1982 enrollment in supplementary schools declined 58 percent nationwide. During the same period enrollment in the Talmud Torah of Minneapolis declined by 38 percent. See *Journal of Jewish Education*, 50, no. 3: 34. For data and analysis of

enrollment trends on the eve of Gordon's appointment as executive director, see Himmelfarb, "Jewish Education for Naught," 1–2.

2. See E. Schwartz, *Moral Education: A Practical Guide for Jewish Teachers* (Denver: Alternatives in Religious Education, 1983), and E. Schwartz, "Three Stages of a School's Moral Development," *Religious Education*, 96, no. 1 (Winter 2001): 106–18.

3. In addition to Harry Malin's coediting of *Model Seder*, Louis E. Newman is author and coauthor of numerous works, including *The Meaning and Practice of T'shuvah* and *Past Imperatives*, Joel Gordon authored a Hebrew primer and is currently editing a series by Noam Zion on Talmudic Narratives about women, Dori Weinstein writes the *Ya-Ya and Yo-Yo* children's series, Phyllis Cytron coauthored *Miriam Mendelow: Mother of Jerusalem* with her husband Rabbi Barry Cytron, and the author.

4. Interview with Rabbi Joel Gordon, February 16, 2015.

5. Gordon, "The Talmud Torah of St. Paul," 20.

6. The Minneapolis Jewish Day School was founded two years after the St. Paul Talmud Torah Day School. Though initially housed at the Minneapolis Talmud Torah, it was not a Talmud Torah program. Similarly, the St. Paul Jewish Community Center would often outshine its counterpart in Minneapolis in the years to come—for example, though Minneapolis agencies had taken tentative steps toward disabilities-inclusive programming in the 1970s, by the 1990s the St. Paul Jewish Community Center's inclusion program was receiving national recognition. Chabad's Cheder elementary school, Bais Chana program for women, and Yeshiva were also founded during this period.

7. Kohlberg took a special interest in the Talmud Torah's moral development curriculum, writing the cover blurb for *Moral Development: A Practical Guide for Jewish Teachers*, the book version of the Rosenthal Moral Development Curriculum. Regarding Kohlberg's connection to Jewish education, see E. Schwartz, "Why Some Ask Why," *Judaism: A Quarterly Journal of Jewish Life and Thought*, 53, nos. 3–4 (Summer–Fall 2004).

8. See B. Cytron and E. Schwartz, *When Life Is in the Balance: Life and Death Decisions in Light of the Jewish Tradition* (New York: United Synagogue, 1986), 194–95.

9. Other Justice Committee/*Vaad Din* preparatory activities included observation of state and federal district court proceedings, conversations with the presiding judges, visits from a St. Paul assistant city attorney, a court-certified ESL Interpreter, an FBI agent, an assistant city and assistant federal district attorney, and a state public defender.

10. The 1983–1984 school year would prove especially contentious. Gordon spent the year on sabbatical in Israel. In his absence, Gavish filled in for Gordon while continuing to direct the rapidly growing Day School. Dissension was especially pronounced in the afternoon program, but the Day School, still in the early stages of constructing and implementing its distinctive integrated curriculum, was also buffeted by criticism from parents.

11. G. Tobin and G. Berger, *Jewish Population Study of Greater St. Paul* (St. Paul: United Jewish Fund and Council of Greater St. Paul, 1993), 8. The study estimated a

total Jewish population of approximately 11,400, of which 24 percent were under the age of 18. See Tobin and Berger, *Jewish Population Study of Greater St. Paul*, 5, 20.

12. Kim Marsh, "Executive Director's Remarks," 50th Annual Meeting of the United Jewish Fund and Council of St. Paul, June 18, 1985. From the author's transcript of the talk.

13. For example, in the 1980s, several families from the Mankato–New Ulm area, 90 miles southwest of the Twin Cities, by-passed closer programs in Minneapolis to bring their children to the Talmud Torah of St. Paul on Sunday mornings.

14. Interview with Harold Smith, May 22, 2015.

15. Raskas mentions Plaut's interest in running for office in a 2005 oral history interview. See "Interview With Rabbi Bernard Raskas," University of Minnesota Libraries, Nathan and Theresa Berman Upper Midwest Jewish Archives, January 2005.

16. Eugene Lipman and Albert Vorspan, eds., *A Tale of Ten Cities* (New York: UAHC, 1962), 287.

17. Regarding East Coast anti-observant mockery, see Eddy Portnoy, *Bad Rabbi* (Palo Alto, CA: Stanford University Press, 2018), 83–88.

18. Minnesota politics from the mid-to-late twentieth century were characteristically progressive, rooted in a fertile mix of socially liberal and culturally traditional tendencies. The role of these regional characteristics in nurturing corresponding forces in Jewish communal life, including Jewish education, has yet to be fully explored, but Elazar had an abiding interest in both subjects. For his observations on aspects of Minnesota social and political cultures in the twentieth century, see D. J. Elazar, V. Gray, and W. Spano, *Minnesota Politics and Government* (Lincoln: University of Nebraska Press, 1999).

19. Daniel J. Elazar, ed., *Jewish Education and Jewish Statesmanship—Albert Elazar Memorial Book* (Jerusalem: Jerusalem Center for Public Affairs, 1996), 1–13.

20. Elazar, *The National-Cultural Movement in Hebrew Education in the Mississippi Valley*, Daniel Elazar On-line Library, http://www.bjpa.org/Publications/details .cfm?PublicationID=2532.

21. The Temple of Aaron, Sons of Jacob, Mt. Zion, and Adath Israel synagogue buildings also date from this period, as do the original George Kaplan Shalom Residence and current Jewish Community Center.

22. Characteristic of this effort, a "*sukkah* on wheels" was parked in "Dinkytown," a student neighborhood adjacent to the University of Minnesota, and students were welcomed in, to shake the "grass" and try on the fringes.

23. The cover of the 1973 anthology *Jewish Radicalism* features a stylized clenched fist with a *magen David* on its palm. The anthologized essays, talks, poetry, and art reflect the political intensity of these developments. See Jack Nusan Porter and Peter Dreier, eds., *Jewish Radicalism* (New York: Grove Press, 1973).

24. Himmelfarb, "Jewish Education for Naught," 11.

25. Benjamin Harshav, *Language in a Time of Revolution* (Berkeley: University of California Press, 1993), viii.

26. Hillel Levine's speech at the meeting of the Council of Jewish Federations and Welfare Funds in Boston, November 1969, "To Share a Vision," originally appeared

in *Response Magazine*, no. 6, 3–10. The talk is also included in Porter and Dreier's *Jewish Radicalism*.

27. Rabbi Mordecai Miller, assistant rabbi at the Temple of Aaron (1974–1981), would also have a strong influence on many leaders of the community in this period, especially through his advocacy of traditional text study.

28. Former executive director Joel Gordon estimated the proportion of Mt. Zion's students enrolled in the supplementary school in the late 1970s and 1980s at roughly 10 percent (Gordon interview, February 8, 2015). Fifteen of the school's 175 students in 1987–1988 were from Mt. Zion affiliated families (Gordon, "A Picture of a Community School," 19). A significant proportion of Day School students would also come from Mt. Zion-affiliated families. As in Minneapolis (until the policy was successfully challenged by Temple Israel), synagogue supplementary programs received no funding from the St. Paul Fund and Council. Implicit in this policy was the premise that synagogue programs, unlike communal agencies, were "private" options.

29. A central figure in the university's Hebrew-related programs throughout this period, Professor Jonathan Paradise, was himself a graduate of the Minneapolis Talmud Torah.

30. CAJE was formally founded in 1977, following a second national conference. In keeping with the spirit of the times, the acronym originally stood for "Coalition for *Alternatives* in Jewish Education." Talmud Torah administrators and faculty played key roles in regional "Minne-CAJE" conferences in the 1980s.

31. Chiat and Proshan, *We Rolled Up our Sleeves*, 88.

32. David Shluker and S. Sterling Epstein, consultants, "JESNA Study of the Talmud Torah of St. Paul, January 22, 1990." The study's curricular recommendations included refocusing the day school curriculum from a "value-oriented" emphasis to greater emphasis on academics, intensification of the Hebrew language program, and improved learning disability services. Regarding the composition of the board, the report recommended that it be reconfigured to include more community members who did not currently have children in a Talmud Torah program, and that it include formal representation from the UJFC.

33. John McCormick, "Kids Tackle Life's Dilemmas," *Minneapolis StarTribune*, May 11, 1991, Section B, 1.

34. Clark Morphew, "Challenges for the Future," *St. Paul Pioneer Press*, April 5, 1996, Section D, 1–2.

35. "Attorney General Humphrey Visits Talmud Torah of St. Paul," *American Jewish World*, March 7, 1997.

36. Cobin shared the story with the author.

37. In the larger community, Catholic parishes and parish schools continued to lend their identity to neighborhoods, contributing to an air of stability and educational focus in the city.

38. Krasner, *The Benderly Boys and American Jewish Education*, 170.

39. One indication of the relative breadth of support the agency enjoyed in this period is the alternating synagogue affiliations of Talmud Torah presidents from 1975 to 2000: 1975–1977, Temple of Aaron; 1977–1979, Sons of Jacob; 1979–1981, Temple of Aaron; 1981–1983, Temple of Aaron; 1983–1985, Temple of Aaron;

1985–1988, Beth Jacob; 1988–1990, Beth Jacob; 1990–1992, Beth Jacob; 1992–1994, Mt. Zion; 1994–1996, Beth Jacob; 1996–1998, Beth Jacob; 1998–2000, Beth Jacob.

40. The new Reform congregation, Shir Tikvah, soon moved to South Minneapolis. Much of the Chabad community remained in close proximity to Adath Israel Synagogue in the city's Highland Park neighborhood, but it too eventually established residential clusters in St. Paul's southern (and Minneapolis' western) suburbs.

41. A Twin Cities havurah-congregation, Shaarei Shalom, was also founded in this period. Though it remained much smaller than other congregations in the Twin Cities and continued to meet in members' homes rather than in a building of its own, it nurtured relationships and leadership skills that would prove significant in the founding of Beth Jacob.

42. Including Talmud Torah faculty, Hillel directors, and staff and faculty members of local colleges.

43. Gordon, "A Picture of a Community School," 19.

44. E.g., B. Talmud, *Sotah* 22b, Rabbi Akiva's disdain for scholars (*P'sahim* 49b), the narrative in *Sefer Hasidim* about a shepherd who is corrected by a scholar regarding the correct form of prayer (J. Wistinetzki edition, 4–6), etc.

45. Krasner's, *Benderly Boys* includes an ample array of condescending and disparaging remarks in this regard.

46. Marjorie Smith Hofman, an afternoon school alumna, was the daughter of Harold and Micky Smith. The Smith family played a key role in the development of the agency.

47. For example, a 1996 Talmud Torah–generated proposal for continued cooperation titled "A Call to Action: A Blueprint for the Talmud Torah of St. Paul" detailed a revised curriculum, greater congregational presence in the school's educational programs, and a procedure for community-wide educational planning. The plan asked in return that the Temple of Aaron "work cooperatively in officially and unequivocally supporting and promoting the Talmud Torah's Afternoon School and Midrasha." Author's copy.

48. Beth Jacob Congregation figures prominently in *Jews in the Center: Conservative Synagogues and Their Members* (New Brunswick, NJ: Rutgers University Press, 2000). While the study references the St. Paul Talmud Torah, it isn't identified as a communal agency, or credited with a primary role in the founding of the congregation, Also, in contrasting Beth Jacob with Beth El Synagogue in Minneapolis, no mention is made of Beth El's origins having been similarly entwined with the Talmud Torah of Minneapolis.

Chapter 3

At the Beginning of the
Twenty-First Century

And then the tidal wave of the Emancipation breaks through. . . . But Jewish education finds itself lagging behind this rapid expansion. The essential change isn't in the undermining of external limits per se. Even before this, the ghetto, though Jewish life welled up within it, didn't close in upon it from all sides. Jews also had interests outside its walls; it was only for the respite and heritage that one went back inside; only there was to be found a *mishkan* for one's spirit. . . .

So, then what has changed? It's that the wanderer doesn't come home in the evening. . . . In other words, one finds a *mishkan* for one's spirit outside the Jewish world.

. . . This time—*talmud torah* in the other direction. This learning no longer goes out from Torah to life, but on the contrary, from life, from the world that does not know of the commandment, or "acts as if doesn't know" the commandment, back to the Torah. This is the identifying sign of the times.

—Franz Rosenzweig ("Notes for Remarks at the
Opening of the Frankfurt Lerhaus," 1920)

By the time the Talmud Torah of St. Paul celebrated its fiftieth anniversary in 2006, much had changed. The St. Paul Jewish community had become, as Kim Marsh predicted, smaller and grayer. Between 1940 and 2000 St. Paul's total population fluctuated between 270,000 and 290,000, while the Jewish population dropped from approximately 14,000 to roughly 11,400 by 1993. A 2004 demographic study, though indicating a relatively stable total number of Jews in St. Paul, showed a decrease of approximately 9 percent in the number of Jewish households in the greater St. Paul area in the years 1994–2004.[1] Along with a general loss of population and households, the median age of the population had risen from approximately thirty-seven in 1992[2] to forty-two by 2004.[3]

The Jewish educational landscape had changed as well. The preceding period had been shaped by strong leaders in the community who shared an overriding commitment to the Talmud Torah as an integrative communal institution and were willing to cooperate on that basis; leaders who understood that a community's most valuable real estate is its common ground. By the mid-1990s, all of these communal positions were held by others. Kim Marsh was no longer executive director of the Fund and Council, others now held the senior rabbi positions in the older congregations (Temple of Aaron and Mt. Zion), the Jewish Community Center would soon have a new executive director, and Rabbi Joel (Yosi) Gordon, a key figure in the agency's growth and its last long-term executive director, had stepped down. After twenty years of relative stability, a period of lapses in communal leadership once again reemerged. The four subsequent Talmud Torah administrators to carry the title "executive director" brought varying aptitudes to the position. However, none of Gordon's successors would demonstrate a comparable combination of Jewish learning, pedagogical skill, and long-term commitment to the local community, nor have a lasting influence on the agency.[4]

In this changed environment, the hopeful expectation of the Fund and Council in 1956 that a central educational agency would go a long way toward "preventing duplication of effort and in promoting efficiency and economy of administration" once again faltered. In the mid-1990s total enrollments in Talmud Torah programs had reached levels not seen since the 1970s, with steadily increasing enrollments in both the Day School and the Afternoon School throughout the early 1990s, and a growing Early Childhood program by the end of the decade as well. Nevertheless, though numbers began to fall in the years that followed, 2000–2001 enrollment in the Day School remained at 185 students, and the Afternoon School at 105, comparable, when combined, to the size of the student body of the Afternoon School immediately prior to the founding of the Day School in 1982. The Talmud Torah also continued to provide the Hebrew language component of Mt. Zion's Religious School, along with some collaborative high school programming.[5] The 2004 Twin Cities Jewish Population Study indicated that 79 percent of respondents very familiar or somewhat familiar with the afternoon program who offered a perception of the school characterized it as good or excellent, while 90 percent of respondents offering a response regarding the Day School indicated an excellent or good perception.[6]

However, the Temple of Aaron's decision to open its own supplementary school would markedly alter the educational climate. The "Community School versus Congregational School" memo included in Harry

Rosenthal's papers had indicated that in the 1950s, as planning of Talmud Torah building on Mississippi River Boulevard proceeded, some Temple of Aaron members continued to believe that "the place of a Talmud Torah is in the synagogue." At the time, support for a community school had prevailed, though the larger significance of the distinction was never fully resolved for some community members, and the proximity of the two institutions no doubt clouded the issue. An often-cited factor in the Temple of Aaron's eventual decision to open its own afternoon program had been the rejection by the Talmud Torah administration of a request by leaders of the congregation that the agency provide a one-afternoon-a-week option. However, the congregation's tentative steps toward opening an early childhood program as well, shortly before launching its afternoon program, despite well-established early childhood divisions at the Jewish Community Center and Talmud Torah, suggested a broader shift in attitudes. When contacted by the American Jewish World about the Temple of Aaron opening its own supplementary program, the response of Rabbi Bernard Raskas, now Rabbi Emeritus of the congregation, was tellingly unenthusiastic. Characterizing the move as "part of the dynamic of change," he concluded, "and whether that change is good or bad only time will tell. I can't predict. I hope it's all for the good."[7]

With the Temple of Aaron's announcement, educational stances in the community began to resemble positions taken in the 1950s, though in some cases held by institutions previously identified with a quite different perspective; in the years that followed, these positions would harden. A 2014 *American Jewish World* advertisement for the Temple of Aaron, which in the 1950s had been the primary congregational supporter of the move toward a central educational agency, now announced that it offered the "Only In-House Conservative Synagogue Religious School."[8]

Daniel Elazar, in his study of communal Jewish educational agencies in the Mississippi Valley, had emphasized the decisive role of synagogue-based challenges to communal educational agencies in undermining their position in community after community. Elazar singled out Minneapolis as illustrative of the ensuing ironies:

In many cases it was the alumni of the Talmud Torahs who founded the Conservative synagogues in the 1920s. For example, the Talmud Torah alumni who had been used to worshipping together while students in a modern atmosphere where the traditional service was maintained with new dignity, decorum, and understanding, continued to worship together and in 1924 founded Beth El, which became the leading Conservative congregation in Minneapolis. There was an irony here in that it was the Conservative movement that came into competition with the Talmud Torahs and led the assault on them on behalf of congregational schools.[9]

Faced with these challenges, the St. Paul Talmud Torah would soon offer high school students the option of enrolling for less than two days (five instructional hours) a week as well. Thus, it seemed, in more and more ways, as the Hebrew saying went, "*Otah ha-g'veret, b'simlah aheret*" (The same lady had returned, if in a different dress).

With the erosion of congregational cooperation, the demise of a shared curricular vision, a competing community day school in Minneapolis (along with Torah Academy, the Lubavitch *Cheder*, and the Minneapolis Talmud Torah), and the end of large-scale emigration from Russia and Eastern Europe to St. Paul, enrollment in all of the St. Paul Talmud Torah programs shrank. The agency's schools strove to sustain their instructional quality and the integrity of their curricula, while strengthening staff and faculty expertise in the areas of physical and learning disabilities. Enrollments, nevertheless, continued to decline, leading to significantly reduced day school and supplementary school programs. The Twin Cities Jewish Middle School closed in 2007, after the St. Paul Talmud Torah and Minneapolis Jewish Day School failed to agree on how an institutional presence could be maintained in both cities, and the early childhood program, the only segment of the Talmud Torah with faculty largely affiliated with the Temple of Aaron, was discontinued in 2013. The details were depressingly familiar: divisions in and between congregations, struggles over focused versus diffused resources, budgetary constraints, disagreements about "authentic" versus "marketable" curricula, and all on top of difficulty sustaining educational cooperation between the Minneapolis and St. Paul communities.

As these changes unfolded, one longtime active member of the St. Paul community would conclude: A new king had arisen over Egypt who hadn't known Joseph.

WHY THE REVERSES?

One could assume that increased educational fragmentation in St. Paul was inevitable, in line with similar developments in other communities across the country. Central communal educational agencies had disappeared in other locales, enrollments in supplementary schools had long been in decline, and by the end of the 1990s the upsurge of day schools also appeared to be at an end.[10] In 1992 Alvin Schiff had predicted, "At the beginning of the next century, when historians and sociologists will scurry to analyze fully the development of the American Jewish community . . . one trend will be clearly outstanding—the phenomenal growth and staying power of Jewish all-day education."[11] However, a decade later, trends would actually look quite different. From 1998 to 2014, non-Orthodox day school enrollment dropped by approximate 8 percent. A 2013–2014 study by the Avi Chai Foundation indicated that the decline was particularly steep among Conservative-affiliated schools. Though the study indicated that community day school enrollments increased from 15,000 to 20,000 students, no doubt due, in part, to the closing of numerous Conservative schools, the social and cultural tailwinds that had driven the rapid expansion of day schools beyond orthodox constituencies were clearly subsiding.[12]

In 1988, buoyed by expectations similar to Schiff's, the Conservative movement's Committee on Jewish Law and Standards endorsed a position paper that indicated a strong preference for schools rooted in Conservative-affiliated synagogues, rather than "community" or cooperative Conservative-Reform sponsored schools. The Avi Chai study would prove a sobering coda to those expectations. But the position paper included a particularly painful message for remaining advocates of communal education. In words resonant with decades of discord, and ironically prescient for St. Paul, it asserted, "Rabbis and synagogues have a stake in trying to root a school in the synagogue rather than a communal agency, since synagogue sponsorship underscores the importance of the synagogue in Jewish life and contributes members and vitality to the sponsoring congregations."[13]

In light of these broad trends, it might seem a foregone conclusion that St. Paul's communal education system would inevitably falter as well. However, given the improbability of the community's successes, a closer look at subsequent setbacks is also warranted. What became of the local idiosyncrasies and timely convergences that had led to those successes?

In 1968, it was estimated that approximately 80 percent of the Jews of Greater St. Paul lived in the city's Highland Park neighborhood, where the Talmud Torah was also located.[14] Among the factors facilitating this residential pattern was the availability of a wide range of housing options in a relatively small area. Strands of large homes stood adjacent to modest bungalows and apartment buildings. The wealthy and those of modest means, business owners and working-class Jews, shared the same streets and commercial outlets, indicative of a relatively compact socioeconomic profile. Unlike in Minneapolis, where the 1960s ended with the precipitous dismantling of Jewish institutions on the city's North Side and their transplantation to scattered sites in the western suburbs, all of St. Paul's communal agencies, congregations, and Jewish-oriented businesses remained within the city limits through the mid-1980s.[15] For a significant proportion of St. Paul Jewish youth, walking with friends and family remained an integral part of synagogue and school attendance, not yet replaced by car rides and parking lots.

In time, residential dispersion would come to St. Paul as well and, with it, receding personal experience of close-knit Jewish neighborhoods. By 2004 it was estimated that only 47 percent of Jews living in greater St. Paul, and

31 percent of Jewish children, lived anywhere within the city limits.[16] A sizable proportion of families living in the suburbs were now located on the outer rim, and the Talmud Torah was no longer providing bus service.

Comparable *cultural* diffusion was reflected in the waning prominence of Jewish languages in the community and their decreasing significance as definitive markers of Jewish identity.[17] Benjamin Harshav had contended that the revitalization of Hebrew was a pivotal factor in the national revival of the Jewish people, but strong affinities for Israel and an associated attachment to Hebrew among younger families could no longer be assumed. Likewise, through the middle of the twentieth century, familiarity with Yiddish had helped to sustain a degree of mutual recognition across diverse segments of the community. Yiddish-speaking Jews, whatever they might eat, or how they parsed their week, were, nevertheless, undoubtedly Jews, even in the eyes of their more observant neighbors. However, by the beginning of the twenty-first century, outside of the Chabad community, Yiddish among St. Paul Jews had largely been reduced to a handful of dog-eared interjections. Absent that idiom—a part of the ambient environment through the middle of the century, even when it was no longer the first language of the majority of community members—the underlying ethnic fabric of the St. Paul community, as elsewhere, wore thin.[18]

In addition, a largely self-contained Chabad community was now the dominant orthodox presence in the city. It, too, had acquired a degree of celebrity during this period, through its Bais Chana program, established in 1971, and the prominence of local Chabad figures.[19] Criticism from Orthodox community members had accompanied the founding of the Talmud Torah, but unlike in the 1950s, when shared ethnic roots, family ties, and commercial relationships kept Orthodox-affiliated families in the communal fold, far fewer crossroads now linked the Chabad community to the rest of St. Paul's Jews. Chabad operated its own schools, and though Chabad teachers occasionally taught in the Talmud Torah's supplementary school, differences in ideology and practice limited broader cooperation. A number of St. Paul's Orthodox-affiliated families had sent their children to the Talmud Torah and served on its staff into the 1970s, but few families from Adath Israel Congregation, led by a Chabad rabbi, now utilized any of the Talmud Torah's programs.

Additionally, an increasing number of Jewish households included parents who as children had little or no Jewish education—parents who had grown up in nominally Jewish homes with little Jewish substance, or in Soviet Bloc countries, or who had become Jews as adults. For these parents, educational choices for their children would not be informed by firsthand childhood experience.

Given these developments, the vague and short-lived slogan "continuity," popularized in federation circles in the 1980s and 1990s, was itself problematic. "Continuity" of what, to what end, and by what measure? Kim Marsh's reference to "creative Jewish continuity" in his 1985 Fund and Council Address was distinguished by his insistence on its substantiation in educational terms, but "continuity" would more commonly serve as an indeterminate cipher.[20]

Other, widespread sociocultural changes had also set in. Jewish leadership at mid-century had been tried and disciplined by the Depression and World War II, stunned by the murder of the Jews of Europe, and revived by the establishment of a Jewish State in the homeland. The cumulative effect of these experiences, each in its own way reinforcing the lesson of strength in unity, was to nurture confidence and perseverance in shared purposes. Despite persistent intra-Jewish differences, especially regarding *halakhah*, a "catholic" sensibility, as Solomon Schechter employed the term, had emerged, attuned to a "collective conscience,"[21] forged by shared experience and still-prevalent cultural bonds. While segments of the next generation, baby-boomers adrift in the backwash of counter-cultural disarray, had sought to further their predecessors' efforts, by the beginning of the twenty-first century that sensibility was rapidly dissipating.[22] As ethnic bonds, shared practices (liturgical, dietary, etc.), intense identification with Israel, and close-knit residential patterns waned, forces that had proven conducive to educational renaissance were dissipating as well.

An illuminating indication of this era-ending shift in the educational environment in St. Paul emerges from a comparison of a 1932 report to the annual meeting of the Jewish Educational Center, St. Paul's first attempt at a communal educational agency, and a 1987 Talmud Torah Education Committee report on the status of the Afternoon School program.[23] The 1932 report, written by Louis Gordon, principal of the Center School, emphasized the need to expand enrollment, to retain students through high school, to make tuition more affordable through community-wide support of the school, to develop broad public appreciation of "the value of a progressive Jewish education," to gain greater parental cooperation in reinforcing the school's curriculum at home, to enhance "extra-curricular activities," and to articulate the crucial role of adult education in the future of the school. Similarly, fifty years later, the 1987 report expressed concern that "the knowledge gained is not being connected to reinforcing activities at home and in the community," that too few of the students continued their studies after celebrating *bar* or *bat mitzvah*, and that the school's informal educational programming needed to be enhanced. While Gordon defined the aim of the school as imbuing its students with "the knowledge and spirit of historic Judaism," the 1987 report indicated that the ultimate goal of the curriculum was to "advance the student in classical Jewish study, stressing the interpretive skills and conceptual content needed to understand and apply knowledge, and to work independently form Hebrew texts." The similarity of concerns and goals in the two reports, despite the intervening years, is striking. In the next several years, however, evidence would emerge indicating that the era defined by the two reports was ending.

BROADER CHANGES

Global changes in climate were clearly affecting the local environment. By the close of the century, a growing proportion of Jews in St. Paul, like Jews throughout the United States, involved themselves in Jewish communal life as selective consumers of communal services. Given this increasingly common orientation, prospects for "marketing" the hours and expense of a substantive education, in under-appreciated competencies, to increasingly evanescent constituencies, especially when congregation-based alternatives seemed sufficient, appeared ever more slim. Commenting on more recent versions of the American penchant for "getting involved," Robert Bellah and coauthors of the much-acclaimed *Habits of the Heart: Individualism and Commitment in American Life* noted that even this seemingly "communal" impulse suggested a peculiarly American notion of the relationship between "self and society":

> Individuals are expected to *get* involved—to choose for themselves to join social groups. They are not automatically involved in social relationships that impose obligations not of their choosing, and social institutions that are not the product of the voluntary choice of the individuals who constitute them are perceived as illegitimate.[24]

In previous generations communal connections were reinforced by relationships forged through small and medium size business relationships—the marketing of this and that—but by the end of the 1990s, "community" itself was coming to be identified as a "market" in connections. Dashefsky and Lazerwitz, using data from the early 1980s, probed a correlation between "affiliation" (with a congregation or two or more Jewish organizations) and increasing numbers of Jews who made a living in professional positions. The data they analyzed, which looked specifically at contributions to the United Jewish Appeal, indicated a "donut" effect in regard to affiliation, with senior executives and professionals more likely to be donors than managers and other professionals, but both groups surpassed by those in sales, clerical and manual positions. Based on this anomaly, Dashefsky and Lazerwitz first suggested that

> many highly educated professionals (e.g., doctors and lawyers) have practices tied to their ethnic community and/or higher incomes necessary for extensive involvement in the community. (Other highly educated professionals, e.g., academicians and scientists are likely to be more integrated into their work community than their ethnic community because they are employed in a bureaucratic organization and are more geographically mobile.)[25]

Though duly cautious about over-generalization, given the study's small sample of respondents, they went on to suggest that along with a higher level of income in the self-employed group, these differences were best explained in terms of self-employment itself:

> Those not self-employed were more likely to be in the *Unaffiliated* group (47 percent) than those self-employed (29 percent). What these findings suggest is that for this sample, formal education was more likely associated with affiliation if the formal education led to a self-employed occupation (e.g., doctor, lawyer, business person).Likewise, the sales, clerical and manual employees may have also been disproportionately self-employed.[26]

Socioeconomic changes in Jewish communities through the middle of the century further exacerbated the challenges faced by educators committed to a communal educational design. Making one's living as a professional employee, a career path increasingly common among Jews by the turn of the century, rather than as an independent professional, or in clerical, sales, or manual positions (which are also more likely to be forms of self-employment), tended to work against institutional affiliation, let alone strong identification with a local community.

However, conscious choices also played a role in the renewed fragmentation of Jewish education in St. Paul. Carving up of the common ground that had made so many successful initiatives possible—ironically, in the name of loyalty to congregations and communal agencies—left the community and its institutions more vulnerable to a dissipating dynamic. The central importance of Jewish learning to Jewish life ensures that places of learning will serve as flash points for conflicting social and ideological forces; forces stirred by broader social influences, ambition or ideology, and the ebb and flow of resources. So, too, in St. Paul. As earlier rabbis and agency heads who had felt sufficiently secure in their positions to advocate for shared communal institutions were replaced by new leaders who focused their efforts on growth within their respective congregations and agencies, the Talmud

Torah's position in the community grew more insecure. In his study of Jewish education in the Mississippi River Valley, Daniel Elazar had stressed the particular role synagogues often played in dissipating support for communal educational agencies:

> The synagogues aggressively and successfully fought to take over Jewish education, killing or attenuating the communal schools in all but two or three communities. None but the very largest congregations could afford full-time professional teachers. They cultivated a profession of educational administrators with part-time teachers, usually poorly trained.[27]

In the 1995 edition of his *Community and Polity*, Elazar returned to the issue, with specific attention to more recent developments in the Twin Cities:

> Finally, there are a handful of full-blown communal school systems—the largest of which in the mid-1990s are located in Minneapolis and St. Paul—that function as the comprehensive educational arms of the Jewish community. . . . These schools are true school systems, integrated vertically and horizontally and maintained with strong federation support. In every case they were able to survive that critical moment after World War II when the challenge of the synagogues was at its height, because of either exceptional leadership or devoted support on the part of a major segment of the community.[28]

In a 1996 St. Paul Pioneer Press article on the Talmud Torah and plans for a middle school, Morris Allen, Rabbi of Beth Jacob Congregation, emphasized the importance of seeing the Talmud Torah Day School in communal terms—a kind of Jewish "public" school—that articulated the community's civic sense of self. The Day School, he said, was "a school of the Jewish community . . . and a responsibility of the Jewish Community."[29] Similarly, Arnold Dashefsky, when queried regarding his repeated references to the communal character of the St. Paul Talmud Torah in pieces published through the end of the century, responded: "Communal Jewish education, as opposed to congregational education, placed the focus on education . . . and not the congregation's religious orientation or ideology."[30] St. Paul community's successful consolidation of supplementary programs into a single communal agency that had grown to include a supplementary school, an early childhood program, a day school, and a well-attended adult education program, and would co-found the Twin Cities Jewish Middle School, was a singular accomplishment. Rather than fostering a patchwork of private and movement-based schools, St. Paul had repeatedly affirmed its communal center, but declining enrollments in the Talmud Torah's programs, concomitant with the reemergence of competing congregation-based programming, now signaled the decline of this Jewish "public" domain.

This transformation could also be seen in the growing number of Jewish children enrolled in magnet, charter, and other-than-Jewish private schools. A symbiotic relationship had long been presumed between public schools and the Talmud Torah supplementary school, with Jewish Day School a reasonable, if ancillary, alternative. But by the first decade of the twenty-first century, both the surge and decline of day school enrollments could no longer be disentangled from greater comfort with varied "private school" options.

As these changes took hold, some pointed to various forms of informal youth programming as fitting alternatives to the curricula employed at the Talmud Torah. Jewish camping in particular, popular in St. Paul as elsewhere in this period, was often cited as an effective response to these developments. However, in addition to questionable educational suppositions regarding formative Jewish learning, "successful" camping posed its own challenges to local Jewish communities. Though camping had the potential to positively influence both campers and staff, its successes could come, ironically, at the expense of identification with the "public" of one's home community, especially when sponsored by national movements intent upon developing their own constituencies. In as much as camping is, by intent and design, a contrived *interruption* of life in one's local community, it posed its own challenges for long-term communal vitality.[31]

These trends made it increasing unclear what St. Paul's Jews might now mean by "Jewish community." As demographic realities made collaboration and "economy of administration" ever more sensible, a cooperative climate was slipping away. In an invited response to a 1992 essay by Jonathan Woocher on "Jewish Education: Crisis and Vision," Joseph Reimer emphasized Woocher's references to the importance of reconnecting Jewish "education" and "community":

> At the heart of Jonathan Woocher's convincing presentation lies his linking of the problems of Jewish education in American today with the problems of American Jewry and the insistence that "the Jewish community must change if any bold vision of what education might be is to come to realization." For as Mordecai Kaplan once argued, it is not schools, but communities that educate. Jewish education can only be as powerful and effective as the sponsoring community allows and wishes it to be.[32]

Neither Woocher nor Reimer discussed in detail the definitive characteristics of "community" they had in mind. They do not associate the construct with residential patterns or other specific features. Reimer introduced the model of the "public school" only to suggest that its ultimate lack of dependence on the active involvement of parents limited its applicability to the challenges of Jewish education, while passing over the idea that a "public" school is, itself, an affirmation of a "public" presence in the educational process, something that would seem to mesh well with his initial emphasis on "community." Moreover, neither writer explored issues raised by seeing a "community" as formed by self-chosen affinities rather than disparate "givens"—generational, socioeconomic, and ideological. Reimer's reference to Mordecai Kaplan was especially noteworthy, as Kaplan's legacy regarding the *locus* of the "communities" he advocated was ambiguous. In St. Paul, in the latter half of the twentieth century, this ambiguity was apparent in the tension between understanding "community" as an inclusive social setting for congregations and other institutions, and contrasting efforts to reinvent congregations as program-rich homes for communal functions. In this respect, Rabbi Morris Katz's criticism of the placement of the first Talmud Torah building adjacent to the new Temple of Aaron building, though perhaps intemperate, was prescient. The proximity had blurred the line between congregation and communal agency among Temple of Aaron members and in the community at large, reinforcing assumptions stemming from the earlier relationship between the congregation and the Center-Capital City School. The disruption of these assumptions in the wake of the Talmud Torah's relocation to Hamline Avenue would add to tensions between the agency and the congregation. While the connection between "community" and "communal educational agency" was proving increasingly successful, the link back from agency to community was coming undone.

In the last quarter of the twentieth century, Jewish life in St. Paul generally, and Jewish education specifically, had reached a position of parity with the larger and wealthier Minneapolis community. However, in the years that followed evidence began to accumulate that in the not so distant future St. Paul's prospects might come to more closely resemble those of Minnesota's third Jewish community, Duluth, where a precipitous decline in the Jewish population was matched by a severe contraction of Jewish communal institutions. By 2014–2015, the Talmud Torah of St. Paul's combined Early Childhood/Day School program had a total of twenty-three students, a decline of approximately 90 percent from the Day School's peak enrollment twenty years earlier. In the years that followed the Day School would fail to reach enrollments sufficient to offer classes beyond second grade.

Supplementary school enrollment faired only slightly better. With a total of sixty-three students, it had shrunk by about 85 percent. Many who might once have been students in one or the other of the Talmud Torah's schools were receiving no formal Jewish education at all, or were now enrolled in one or two day-a-week synagogue programs that fell far short of the academic depth that had been available through the Talmud Torah's day school or supplementary school in their prime. Decline in enrollments, in turn, lead to comparable cuts in faculty and staff. Some of these reductions were acrimonious, but contentious or not, the contraction of the faculty further attenuated the agency's presence and standing in the community.

An era of focused utilization of Jewish educators, facilities, and financial resources had amply demonstrated the importance of collaboration. Dramatic educational advances had pointed the way to a future the community's other institutions could build upon—but not construct on their own. The community could no more afford a disjointed proliferation of programs in the twenty-first century, socially or financially, than it could in the 1940s and 1950s. Nevertheless, a period of relative consensus regarding "community" as the optimum context for Jewish education in St. Paul was passing. The Avi Chai study had found that "community" day school enrollment nationally was actually continuing to grow, but parlaying that trend in St. Paul depended on widespread commitment to shared communal institutions. Absent leaders whose institutional ties were grounded in devotion to the community as a whole, the same advantages of relative size that had facilitated innovation and agile planning in St. Paul now threatened to exacerbate the problems of a shrinking and graying community. Why, after all, would committed young Jews and Jewish families, bearers of the revitalization the St. Paul Jewish community so badly needed, chose to make their home in a community that had allowed such promise to slip away?

NOTES

1. Tobin and Berger, *Jewish Population Study of Greater St. Paul*, 5. I. Sheskin, *2004 Twin Cities Jewish Community Study* (Minneapolis–St. Paul: Minneapolis Jewish Federation, United Jewish Fund and Council of St. Paul, 2005), i. The latter study indicated a total Jewish population of 10,900 in the St. Paul metropolitan area. A 2010 update of the 2004 study indicated an additional 9.8 percent decline in population.

2. Tobin and Berger, *Jewish Population Study of Greater St. Paul*, 21.

3. Sheskin, *2004 Twin Cities Jewish Community Study*, 43.

4. A sense of the devotion the institution inspired can also be seen in the skilled assistance provided by several interim volunteer administrators following Gordon's departure.

5. Talmud Torah of St. Paul 2000–2001 Budget Presentation Packet (prepared for the United Jewish Fund and Council of St. Paul), 4.

6. Sheskin, *2004 Twin Cities Jewish Community Study*, 9–106, 9–111.

7. Marshall Hoffman, "Temple of Aaron School Decision Riles St. Paul Jews," *American Jewish World*, January 14, 2000, 1.

8. *American Jewish World*, August 13, 2014, Education Section. A few inches above the advertisement, an article reported that the local Humanistic Congregation was moving its "Jewish Cultural School" to the Talmud Torah of St. Paul's building.

9. Elazar, *The National-Cultural Movement in Hebrew Education in the Mississippi Valley* (Daniel Elazar On-line Library). http://www.bjpa.org/Publications/details.cfm?PublicationID=2532, Elazar's observations have significant implications for the study of synagogues as well as schools, but are often overlooked, for example, Marc Lee Raphael's, *The Synagogue in America* (New York: NYU Press, 2010), which only discusses in-house synagogue educational programs.

10. The Talmud Torah of Minneapolis's profile also continued to wane. Once considered among the most distinguished of communal educational agencies, it came to be associated almost exclusively with the community's Conservative congregations by the end of the century. In 2014 its elementary program came under the aegis of Minneapolis's two Conservative congregations, and its high school/*Bet Midrash* was discontinued, to make way for the newly formed "Yachad" educational program. Other institutional partners in Yachad included the Minneapolis non-Orthodox Day School, the Minneapolis Federation, Community Center, Conservative and Reform congregations, and a progressive orthodox congregation. Torah Academy, Bais Yaakov Girls School, the Minneapolis Yeshiva, and the two remaining orthodox congregations did not join the initiative. By 2018, one of the synagogue partners had left the partnership, and despite its largely undemanding course offerings, enrollments had dramatically declined.

11. Kelman, *What We Know About Jewish Education*, 149.

12. *A Census of Jewish Day Schools 2013–2014* (Avi Chai Foundation), Marvin Schick project director.

13. David J. Fine, ed., *Responsa: 1980–1990* (New York: Rabbinical Assembly, 2005), 330.

14. Dashefsky and Shapiro, "The Jewish Community of St. Paul," 1971.

15. Between 1957 and 1971, 94 percent of Jews living in North Minneapolis moved away, mostly to the Western suburbs. See John Adams and Barbara Van Drasek, *Minneapolis–St. Paul: People, Places and Public Life* (Minneapolis: University of Minnesota Press, 1993), 75.

16. Sheskin, *2004 Twin Cities Jewish Community Study, Preliminary Results* (Graphical Summary), 14.

17. The original language of instruction in St. Paul's supplementary programs (with the exception of the Mount Zion's Religious School) was Yiddish, including instruction in Hebrew and rabbinic Aramaic.

18. Yosi Gordon would illustrate the point with a story about one of his Talmud Torah in the 1980s who, upon coming across the word "נו?/Nu?" in a passage in a Hebrew language textbook, asked for a translation.

19. In its early stages, the local Lubavitch community was led by North Minneapolis native and Talmud Torah of Minneapolis alumnus Rabbi Moshe Feller. Feller continued to figure prominently in the local Lubavitch community, though much of its subsequent leadership and membership has not had local roots. His personal background undoubtedly played an important role in establishing connections and cultivating positive regard for his efforts.

20. The author served on the Continuity Committee of the St. Paul Fund and Council in the early 2000s. The committee's charge did not include a working definition of "continuity."

21. Solomon Schechter, *Studies in Judaism* (Philadelphia: JPS, 1958), 15.

22. The Pew Study, "A Portrait of Jewish Americans," October 2013, clearly evidenced these developments. See http://www.pewforum.org/2013/10/01/jewish-american-beliefs-attitudes-culture-survey/.

23. Principal's Report, Annual Meeting of the Jewish Education Center Association, May 24, 1932; Education Committee Report to the Talmud Torah Board of Directors, November 4, 1987. Gordon's comments were found in the Talmud Torah of St. Paul Archives, attached to the 1987 Education Committee report and the agenda of the Board of Directors Meeting at which it was presented. It seems likely that the inclusion of the Gordon's 1932 report with the 1987 Education Committee report was intended to demonstrate the long-standing nature of salient issues.

24. Robert Bellah, Richard Madsen, William Sullivan, Ann Swidler, and Steven Tipton, *Habits of the Heart* (New York: Perennial, 1985), 167.

25. A. Dashefsky and B. Lazerwitz, *Charitable Choices: Philanthropic Decisions of Donors in the American Jewish Community* (Lanham, MD: Lexington Books, 2009), 62.

26. Dashefsky and Lazerwitz, *Charitable Choices*, 62.

27. Elazar, *The National-Cultural Movement in Hebrew Education in the Mississippi Valley.*

28. Elazar, *Community and Polity*, 283. In addition to challenges from synagogues, Elazar suggested that the increasing number of day schools also posed a challenge to communal Talmud Torahs. He specifically notes St. Paul in the regard (loc. cit.).

29. Morphew, "Challenges for the Future."

30. Personal correspondence with the author (December 19, 2014) regarding Dasheksky's persistent emphasis of this point, e.g., the endnote in his chapter on "Jewish Identification" in the anthology *What We Know About Jewish Education*" (p. 112, note 3): "In St. Paul, at the time of the study, the community supported one central school system, the Talmud Torah." He makes the same observation in "Does Jewish Schooling Matter?" *Contemporary Jewry*, 23, no. 1 (December 2002): 122, note 5.

31. Dashefsky and Lazerwitz contended that long-term influences of Jewish camping on Jewish identification, as compared to formal Jewish education, had not yet been clearly documented. Specifically, the data they analyzed didn't indicate a strong correlation between camping or youth group experience and affiliation. In fact, a positive correlation with affiliation was stronger for those with *no* Jewish camping experience (Dashefsky and Lazerwitz, *Charitable Choices*, 63–65). The 2011 study "Camp Works: The Long-Term Impact of Jewish Overnight Camping," by Cohen, Miller, Sheskin and Torr, using more recent data, contests this conclusion.

32. David A. Teutch, ed., *Imagining the Jewish Future: Essays and Responses* (Albany: State University of New York Press, 1992), 78.

Chapter 4

The St. Paul Jewish Community Planning Process

... and make boards for the *mishkan* ...

—Exodus 26:15

But where did the boards come from? Jacob, our father, planted them. As he was traveling down to Egypt he said to his children: "Children! It is going to happen that you will be liberated from this place, and it is going to happen that after you have been liberated the Holy One Who is Blessed will tell you to make a *mishkan*. So, get up and plant cedars now, so that when God tells you to make a *mishkan* the cedars will be ready for you." They immediately got up and planted them. That is what it means when it says "boards"—the ones their ancestors readied for them.

—*Tanhuma*, Parashat T'rumah

In 2012 the Jewish Federation of Greater St. Paul (formally "United Jewish Fund and Council") initiated a "Jewish Community Planning Process" to clarify "what the Jewish community is thinking, what topics are on peoples' minds."[1] The language used to describe the Planning Process was measured, but the concerns that led to it were pressing, beginning with the all too evident aging and shrinking of the community that Kim Marsh had foreseen some thirty years earlier. Other studies and planning committees—the 1935 education study, the Fund and Council's Social Planning Committee in the 1940s, the 1978 AAJE study—had played important roles in helping the community to foresee and negotiate transitional challenges. The Community Planning Process would inherit this charge, along with the challenges.

The public portion of the Planning Process was launched in 2013 with thirty-seven listening sessions held at various locations in St. Paul and surrounding suburbs. Approximately 350 community members, 3.8 percent of the population by the researchers' calculation, participated.[2] Responses regarding the assets, needs, and goals of the St. Paul community were gathered from moderated small group discussions and questionnaires. Analysis of the responses by a Planning Committee led to the framing of a "Guiding Principle and Goal" and "Five Priorities."

THE GUIDING PRINCIPLE AND GOAL

To engage all St. Paul agencies, institutions and synagogues to build a vibrant, cohesive, and inclusive Jewish community in Greater St. Paul. To be successful, lay and professional leaders will intentionally work together in ever-increasing collaboration and with a common purpose.

THE FIVE PRIORITIES

1. Build the foundation of community
2. Engage the next generation
3. Inspire giving (create the commitment to financially sustain the community's institutions)
4. Strengthen Jewish education
5. Enhance cooperation (between St. Paul and Minneapolis Jewish communities)[3]

A century of accomplishment and discord, especially in the area of Jewish education, was discernible at the roots of the Planning Process goals and priorities. The "Guiding Principle and Goal" centered on institutional collaboration, as did Priority 5, while Priorities 2 and 4 related directly to Jewish education. Significantly, the most common "issue" or "concern" voiced by listening session participants was "Availability, Quality and Responsiveness of Jewish Education and Social Services (24%)."[4] If there was anything revealing about the findings it was the extent to which concerns and frustrations commonly voiced by educators were widely shared by other community members as well. In highlighting the need for greater institutional collaboration and a community-wide focus on education, the listening sessions returned to contested ground community members had had good reason to believe was behind them. A year earlier the federation had convened a "Jewish Education Collaboration Initiative," intended to bring together "our community agencies and synagogues to explore new ways of working together to offer our children the best possible Jewish education,"[5] but the effort faltered and dissolved along synagogue lines. The Community Planning Process would face similar obstacles, but the finding that these issues remained of concern to so many was also reason for hope.

Having identified communal goals and priorities, Planning Process leaders assembled panels to formulate communal objectives for the prioritized areas, including a panel on how to "strengthen Jewish education." Among the members of the education panel were the senior rabbis of the community's Conservative and Reform congregations, but it would not include Chabad or Adath Israel Congregation representatives. The executive director of the St. Paul Federation also occasionally sat in on meetings, but, initially, the Talmud Torah was not formally represented on the panel. When this was noted at the panel's first meeting in May 2015, it was agreed that a Talmud Torah representative also would be invited to participate.

The panel's first meeting was a promising beginning. The group didn't convene again until the fall, but a series of meetings in rapid succession in October and November proved fruitful. In time, the panel would come to focus its efforts on crafting a proposal for a collaborative supplementary eighth-through-twelfth-grade program. Several considerations recommended such a goal:

1. Research had repeatedly indicated the pivotal role of the high school years in effective Jewish education.[6]
2. Congregational programs were less likely to include faculty with the expertise necessary for substantive learning at the high school level.
3. Success establishing a program specific to the high school years would build confidence in the planning process and encourage broader educational initiatives.
4. A joint Talmud Torah-Mt. Zion Congregation High School program was already in place.
5. Congregational education programs, to the extent that they are used to attract and retain members, tend to be focused on families with young children. A communal high school program was less likely to challenge this objective.

Seen in this light, the decision to focus first on a high school program was a sensible response to the panel's charge. Nonetheless, initial efforts to craft a plan for the program exposed underlying procedural weaknesses, beginning with the absence of shared premises. The panel's "Guidelines," for example, specified that its work would be "community oriented." However, the instructions came without a working definition of "community."

When this lacuna was noted, a subcommittee was formed to determine an applicable definition.

The need to clarify the meaning of so basic a term as "community" underscored the challenges the planners faced, and throughout the process the panel would continue to revisit related, basic questions: What are the definitive characteristics of Jewish education? What constitutes a successful Jewish educational program? How is Jewish educational success measured? What is the optimal relationship between a communal educational program and the community's congregations? What would be the best setting for such a program, and under whose aegis? Given that the community already had an educational agency with middle school and high school classes, and a strong, underused facility, why wouldn't the Talmud Torah be the obvious starting point for such an effort? And perhaps most troubling and revealing: Would children of families not affiliated with a congregation be welcome?

Eventually, the subcommittee given the task of providing a definition of "community" would conclude that in as much as the panel had been convened at the behest of the Federation, and was accountable to it, "community" should be understood as the Federation used the term: broadly, inclusively, and above and beyond particular institutional affiliations and ideological inclinations. Nevertheless, progress remained erratic; a year and a half into the panel's work, an outside consultant was retained to assist in completing planning of the new program. The consultant's work soon focused on helping the participating congregational rabbis and a representative of the Talmud Torah to arrive at a plan among themselves that could be brought back to the panel and their respective constituencies for ratification. However, this more concentrated effort, rather than expediting matters, further slowed the process, as obvious solutions to practical problems—for example, locating the program in its first year at the Talmud Torah—were vetoed. As the process dragged on, it became increasingly clear that the initiative was caught up in circumstances the St. Paul community had not faced since the 1940s, as educational planning was once again fully factionalized on congregational grounds.

In the course of its deliberations, the consultant and working group hammered out a *brit* (covenant) of broad guidelines governing the development of the proposed high school program. By mid-2017 the boards of directors of all three participating congregations, the Talmud Torah, and the St. Paul Federation, had ratified the agreement, but the document gave no indication of continued support of a communal educational agency, nor of curricular expectations. Its vague and hesitant tone signaled how far the covenantal arc had fallen.[7]

In yet another move to advance the process, a "transition team" of three representatives from each of the participating congregations, and two from the Federation and the Talmud Torah, was assembled in the fall of 2017 and assigned the task of finalizing plans for the new program. While this seemed, on the surface, a significant step forward, the transition team's structure and mission reflected the same collision of interests that had dogged the process from its inception, and it would now join the education panel in revisiting basic questions, with definitions adopted and suspended, a start date for a new program set, and then set back—purposes narrowed and process lengthened; agreement reached and retracted. The process would carry on this way until February 2018, when the Federation issued a statement indicating that the effort was at an end, as the challenges had proven, for the time being, insurmountable. Significantly, the same announcement also noted that at the Federation board meeting, less than a week after the last meeting of the transition team, a motion was passed stating: "The Federation will form a task force to study education funding in St. Paul and make recommendations on whether to change the funding and if so how."[8]

Difficulties engaging and working through such questions were increasing reminiscent of the fitful planning initiatives of the 1930s and 1950s, when education had also proven a major source of tension between congregations and communal institutions. But there was one crucial difference. In those earlier decades, efforts had been buoyed, despite all, by a growing confidence that communal cohesion, focused use of resources, educational excellence (rooted in the Hebrew language and classical texts), and cultural renewal (sparked by a fertile mingling of traditional Jewish and American values) were all within reach, while such expectations were now commonly viewed as something that once was. If the community were to demonstrate a renewed capacity to overcome such divisions, St. Paul's story would continue to be of importance to similarly divided localities, and of some lasting significance as well. Yield to those forces, and St. Paul's educational profile would soon resemble that of Minneapolis and other communities where high aspirations and achievement had given way to resignation.

Assuming then, that "community" is to be understood in the broad, trans-congregational terms initially affirmed by the Planning Panel, what light might the history of Jewish education in St. Paul cast on current educational planning in the Twin Cities and other communities facing similar challenges? What does this history suggest is required of communities committed to communal education, understood in these terms? Part II begins with interviews of six educators who played a crucial role in shaping the institutional structure, culture and curricula of the Talmud Torah of St. Paul. The interviews are followed by a description of current circumstances and analysis of what revitalizing communal education in St. Paul would likely entail.

NOTES

1. Jewish Federation of St. Paul Community Planning Process Findings, Executive Summary, March 4, 2014, 4.

2. The Planning Committee identified the largest underrepresented group in the sample as "unaffiliated with a synagogue." Other groups also identified as underrepresented were youth, members of Reconstructionist and Humanist congregations, and households with members who are not Jewish. Community Planning Process Findings, Executive Summary, 8.

3. St. Paul Jewish Federation Community Planning Process, *Priority 4: Strengthen Jewish Education*, Final Report. St. Paul: Jewish Federation of Greater St. Paul, October 2018, 6.

4. Community Planning Process Findings, Executive Summary, 14. Other issues and concerns noted in the Executive Summary, in order of declining prevalence, were as follows: community exclusivity and unsatisfactory outreach to other Jews; assimilation and changes in Jewish values, beliefs, and practices; division and lack of cooperation between Jewish organizations and communities; changes in Jewish population size, attributes, and mobility; high cost of tuition, membership, and services; strategic planning and fund raising; perceptions of prejudice and discrimination (p. 15).

5. *Connections Magazine*, "UJFC of St. Paul," Fall 2011, 1.

6. Most recently, the "Strategic Directions for Jewish Life: Call to Action" statement, published in *Jewish Philanthropy* in October 2015 advocated focusing educational energies on the high school years: "The most promising approach focuses on adolescent Jewish education . . . day schools, supplementary schools, overnight Jewish camps, Israel trips, and youth groups. These experiences, taking place in the crucial identity-forming high school years, work in synergy. They support one another, and recruit for one another." http://ejewishphilanthropy.com.

7. For the text of the *Brit*, see Appendix II.

8. Jewish Federation of Greater St. Paul Board of Directors Meeting Minutes, Tuesday, February 27, 2018. https://cdn.fedweb.org/fed-103/2627/Board%2520Minutes%25202-27-18.pdf.

Part II

Chapter 5

Hindsight and Foresight

Despite this adversity, there are significant developments which I
believe to be the harbingers of our future success.

—Kim Marsh, executive director,
St. Paul United Jewish Fund and Council, 1985

An educational program's "success" is typically measured on the basis of
two criteria: enrollments and academic achievement—that is, who enters the
school and who leaves. However, when speaking of a school's "success"
in communal terms, that is, in terms of what an educational institution can
contribute to the vitality and integrity of its community, as was Kim Marsh's
intent, these criteria are inadequate. The success of a school in *communal*
terms cannot be gauged simply by the size of its student body, or the individual success of its students. Over and above these markers, the degree to
which a school conveys the needs and aspirations of its community, prepares
students to meet those needs and aspirations, and inspires responsive faculty
members, students, and families also must be assessed. Grappling with these
goals is difficult enough in periods of relative cultural stability, but all the
more so as shared criteria for judging the appropriate contours of community
are eroding; it is increasingly difficult as consensus regarding the proper
measure of a community's "vitality," "integrity," and "success" slips away,
and there is little agreement regarding the purposes or character of a Jewish
education.

As memories of educational collaboration in St. Paul receded, pride in the
ensuing accomplishments faded as well. By the beginning of the twenty-first
century, a significant proportion of the community could not, or would not,
recall what all the excitement around Jewish education in St. Paul had been

85

about. With this in mind, six educators who played key roles in shaping one or more of the Talmud Torah's schools during the community's period of greatest educational vitality were interviewed regarding what "strengthening Jewish education," "enhancing intergenerational engagement," and "building the foundation of community"—all St. Paul Community Planning Process goals—entailed in the recent past and will require in the future.[1] Interviewed in early 2015, Rabbi Yosi Gordon, Ruth Gavish (by correspondence and in person), Susan Cobin, Cindy Reich, Sara Lynn Newberger, and Dalia Vlodaver were each asked to reflect on the circumstances that led to the exceptional educational successes of the period, developments in the community in more recent years, and prospects for the future. Their range of experience, accomplishments, and areas of expertise make them especially well qualified for the task. The group includes a Covenant Award winner, a nationally known educational consultant, a Jerusalem Fellow, and a founding faculty member of American Hebrew Academy. They come with extensive teaching and administrative experience in Israel and the United States, and include parents, grandparents, and nonparents of Talmud Torah students; residents of both Minneapolis and St. Paul at the time they were employed by the Talmud Torah; and affiliates of one Orthodox and several Conservative congregations. Summaries of the interviews are given further.

DALIA VLODAVER

Dalia Vlodaver was born in Petah Tikvah, Israel, and taught in several secondary schools in Israel before coming to St. Paul in 1970. During her first two years at the Talmud Torah (1971–1973), she also taught Hebrew at Highland Park Senior High School. In 1995, having served on the afternoon school faculty for over twenty years, Vlodaver was appointed principal of the afternoon school, retiring from the position in 2006.

Having begun her work at the Talmud Torah in the early years of Harry Malin's tenure as executive director, Vlodaver's interview was informed by a longer personal connection to the school than any of the other interviewees. Nevertheless, her observations would closely resemble conclusions voiced by the others. Reflecting on educational successes, she emphasized substantive teaching and learning. She credited Rabbi Yosi Gordon in particular with having built on Harry Malin's success in building an able and enthusiastic faculty. Gordon, she observed, appreciated the importance of providing faculty with ample opportunities to grow in their learning and teaching skills. Vlodaver also confirmed the impression, frequently expressed by other educators and communal leaders, that the community's most influential figures from the 1960s through the early 1990s, despite denominational differences, shared a firm commitment to educational collaboration and consequential learning.

Asked about prospects for the future, Vlodaver was direct: "This isn't just our past, it's our future. And otherwise - " Vlodaver left the alternative unspoken, concluding instead with the hope that both the Day School and Talmud Torah Afternoon School would continue to receive adequate support to sustain what she characterized as their "vital" roles in the community.

RABBI JOEL GORDON

Rabbi Joel (Yosi) Gordon grew up in Green Bay, Wisconsin. He attended the University of Wisconsin, Madison, and received his rabbinical *s'mikhah* from the Jewish Theological Seminary. Before coming to St. Paul, Gordon was the assistant director of Los Angeles Hebrew High School.

He served as the executive director of the Talmud Torah from 1978 to 1990, the longest term of service in the position and the last to extend beyond a few years. Following his tenure as director, he has been a faculty member of the St. Paul Talmud Torah Day School and Afternoon School, the Twin Cities Jewish Middle School, and the Talmud Torah of Minneapolis. Gordon was a 2000 recipient of a Covenant Award for Outstanding Jewish Educators.

Asked about the factors he believed most significantly contributed to the flourishing of Jewish education in St. Paul in the 1980s and 1990s and the Talmud Torah's role in that process, Rabbi Gordon connected the institution's exceptional growth and curricular development with a "unified community" and a talented and effective faculty. In his 1988 article on the Talmud Torah as a model for successful community schools, Gordon had emphasized community-wide cooperation and a corresponding embrace of communal diversity by the agency as key factors in that success, and he strongly reiterated these points in the interview. He also stressed the importance of effective leadership of the Talmud Torah as a whole, as well as in each of its schools. While the individual programs continued to enjoy such leadership in the years that followed, the absence of a long-term executive director with expert educational skills, whose attention was fully focused on continued development of the institution as a whole, seriously undermined continued growth. Gordon acknowledged a changed demographic profile and social dynamic in the community. He believed, however, that with stronger leadership in more recent decades, the Talmud Torah might have more effectively met those changes, including renewed synagogue territorialism.

Regarding an educational agenda for the years to come, Gordon was frankly skeptical of the future of the Day School, but foresaw more promising possibilities for the afternoon school, perhaps including a program located on a rotating basis in the community's synagogues. He also envisioned the development of a volunteer community educators corps that might help Talmud Torah students to bridge gaps in attendance due to increasingly unwieldy schedules.

RUTH GAVISH

Ruth Gavish, like Dalia Vlodaver, was born in Petah Tikvah, Israel. Gavish taught in Israel's *"mam'lakhti/*public" school system before coming to the United States, where she continued to work in Jewish education. She was the assistant director of the Talmud Torah from 1980 to 1982, and principal of the Day School from 1982 to 1986. Gavish exerted the greatest influence on the culture and educational framework of the Day School in its formative years. Subsequent to her work in St. Paul, she continued to serve in Jewish educational positions, including at American Hebrew Academy, in Greensboro North Carolina, where she established the Hebrew language program. Her comments focused primarily on the Day School.

Gavish emphasized six accomplishments of the Day School in its early years:

1. It successfully overcame fears of a return to Jewish "parochialism."
2. It pioneered an innovative, richly experiential, and fully integrated Jewish/general curriculum.
3. It articulated for families, faculty, and staff alike a full range of communal functions: "We worked as a team, we planned, we celebrated, we sang, we laughed, we cried . . ."
4. School life was permeated by a deep and rich Jewish ethos, involving many parent volunteers who worked and learned alongside their children.
5. It succeeded in developing a generation of inspired students *and* faculty.
6. It contributed significantly to the invigoration of Jewish life in the community at large.

Regarding characteristics of the community that she believed facilitated these developments, Gavish noted that even doubts regarding the viability of a communal Day School initially worked to the school's advantage by taking some of the pressure off the founders to meet preconceived expectations. She also suggested that the active involvement of Jews in St. Paul's many colleges and universities was indicative of a positive orientation toward excellent education in general.

Gavish also credited the particular group of educators and administrators then at the Talmud Torah, their love of teaching and Jewish life, their respect for one another, and their capacity to work collaboratively. In practical terms, Gavish noted that being able to provide bus transportation to students from Minneapolis was a significant plus. In addition, the advantages of being a part of a larger communal agency, along with enjoying the ready assistance of St. Paul's other agencies and synagogues, were important factors in the school's early success.

SUSAN COBIN

Before coming to the Talmud Torah, Susan Cobin worked in a number of educational settings, including a local public high school. She was the principal of the Talmud Torah Day School from 1987 to 1998, and principal of the Twin Cities Jewish Day School from its inception through 2006. From 2013 to 2016 she returned to the Day School to serve as interim principal.

Cobin expressed the hope that the student body of the Day School (now the Newman School) might grow through enrollments from both inside and outside the Jewish community, noting that the curriculum had been modified to make the school more attractive to non-Jewish families. The example of the Lippman School in Akron, Ohio, strongly influenced these modifications. Situated in a community in some respects similar to St. Paul, the Lippman School offers global studies and music tracks, in addition to its Jewish studies program.

Reflecting on past successes of all the Talmud Torah's programs, Cobin first noted the strong financial support of the Jewish Federation of Greater St. Paul and the budgetary and staffing benefits of sharing personnel, finances, and other material resources among Talmud Torah programs in the 1980s and 1990s. She then went on to single out four additional strengths of the Day School and Middle School in particular:

1. Successfully attracting and effectively integrating students and families of diverse Jewish background and orientations, including intermarried families and families with one Jewish parent and one recently Jewish parent, with limited Jewish experience or skills;
2. Serving as a point of access to the Jewish community and a setting for communal solidarity for Jewish families unfamiliar or uncomfortable with other ways of Jewish involvement and affiliation;
3. Cultivating strong academic achievement in both Jewish and general studies. Along with an approach to the study of classical Jewish texts that nurtured broadly applicable analytical skills, Cobin also emphasized highly developed fine arts and intercultural awareness components of the curriculum;

4. Stimulating personal growth and learning among staff and faculty members, especially as a result of working closely with students and families who often had backgrounds significantly different from their own.

Faced with much lower enrollments in the remaining Talmud Torah programs, Cobin acknowledged that numbers matter, both pedagogically and in terms of communal impact. Nevertheless, she concluded, enrollment numbers alone should not drive discussion of the future of the agency and its schools. Rather, the four qualitative measures of success noted above should remain primary considerations in ongoing educational planning by and for the community.

SARA LYNN NEWBERGER

Sara Lynn Newberger hails from Chicago. Before coming to the Talmud Torah in 1989, she had extensive experience in informal Jewish education and was a Jerusalem Fellow. She has been an administrator and faculty member of Talmud Torah programs, serving as Day School curriculum coordinator and principal, principal of the Afternoon School, Twin Cities Jewish Middle School Jewish Studies instructor, and director of the Talmud Torah's current *Hineni* adult education program.

When asked to characterize the nature of the Talmud Torah's past "successes," Newberger pointed to four factors:

1. Excellent school leadership and excellent faculties.
2. A clearly articulated mission: "Everyone knew what the place was about"—including the students.
3. Broad-based support from the community's rabbis. Newberger noted in this regard that at one point a single Day School class of approximately fifteen students included the children of five Conservative and Reform rabbis.
4. Mutually reinforcing congregation-school relationships and experiences.

Turning to the future, Newberger focused on prospects for the Day School. Her expectations remained rooted in the academic vision that had shaped the school in its formative years. However, even with revived interest in such a curriculum and effective outreach, she foresaw a much smaller school of perhaps 60 to 70 students in grades K–5. Much would depend, she suggested, on the strength of the pride in the school she still sensed in the community. Could that pride be catalyzed on the Talmud Torah's behalf? That, she concluded, remained to be seen.

CINDY REICH

Cindy Reich, born and raised in Philadelphia, Pennsylvania, came to the Talmud Torah with an extensive background in Jewish education. Having completed her PhD in evaluation studies, she has gone on to serve as an educational consultant in a number of locales across the country. Reich was a member of the Day School faculty prior to serving as its principal from 1998 through 2006 and her comments focused primarily on the Day School.

When asked to assess the accomplishments of the Day School from the late 1980s through the end of her term as principal, Reich noted:

1. Success in "community building" among families and students;
2. Developing the students' critical thinking skills;
3. Developing the students' commitment to social justice;
4. Providing personal and meaningful access to Jewish sources;
5. Fostering artistic growth.

Reflecting on the basis of these achievements, Reich noted two demographic factors that had worked in the St. Paul Day School's favor: (1) the influx of students from the former Soviet Union, and (2) proximity to Minneapolis, where the non-Orthodox day school was slow in achieving a comparable reputation. With the end of large-scale immigration from the former Soviet Union, the continued move of Minneapolis Jews and Jewish institutions westward, away from St. Paul, and growing regard for the Minneapolis Jewish Day School, these factors no longer favored enrollment in St. Paul Talmud Torah programs.

Reich also noted a cultural shift in the community toward a greater emphasis on ensuring that Jewish children fully participate in the "larger world." This, along with the expense of a Day School education, the inconvenience of school-related commuting, and demographic changes in the community, led to decreasing enrollments.

Regarding future prospects for "success," Reich was circumspect. All of the factors that had contributed to declining enrollments would need to be addressed. She emphasized in this regard the importance of strong supportive communal leadership, but she also noted that the school's curriculum and culture would need to prove as attractive and responsive to current parental inclinations as had the curricula of the 1980s and 1990s. Given the scarcity of resources, the shrinking size of the community, and that "funders are looking for collaboration," institutional cooperation would be as important as ever, including cooperation with institutions in Minneapolis. Even so, Reich concluded, maybe "success" and "failure" were the wrong categories. Alluding to Rawidowicz and the "last Jews," she concluded that "everything evolves," even when it might feel, at the time, like failure.

The interviewees' observations about past successes cluster around six familiar themes:

1. Fortuitous demographic factors.
2. Excellent Talmud Torah leadership at both the agency and program level.
3. Supportive communal leadership, especially among congregational rabbis and agency directors.
4. Schools serving as a "community" for some, and augmenting and enhancing community life for others; in either case, having an integrative role in the larger Jewish community.
5. Strong faculties, capable of cultivating academic excellence.
6. A clear mission for each program, understood and shared by administrators, faculty members, and families, that earned the esteem of the larger community.

The interviewees agreed that the accomplishments of the 1980s and 1990s were real, and, in many respects, exceptional, but tended to be skeptical about prospects for sparking a comparable educational resurgence at this point in the agency's and community's history. Concerns were especially pronounced regarding the Day School. Those interviewed found a resurrection of the Day School of the 1980s and 1990s unlikely, and disagreed about the feasibility or appeal of other models. Specifically, recent modifications in the day school curriculum noted by Susan Cobin have not coincided with renewed growth in the student body beyond the primary grades, which has, in turn, precluded their full implementation. There was agreement, however, that not only would an educational resurgence require the convergence of the factors that had led to earlier successes, but that the effort would have to gain momentum much more quickly. Contentious decades had preceded those earlier achievements. Current demographic and cultural trends would not allow for a comparably long and twisting path to cooperation and revitalization.

None of the educators expressed second thoughts about bringing several programs together under the same institutional roof nor the emphasis that had been placed on the development of classical competencies (Hebrew language skills, facility with classical Jewish texts, liturgical skills) along with a systematic focus on the development of moral judgment. However, it was commonly acknowledged that success in the future would require that the respective curricula continue to grow and adapt to changed circumstances.

Finally, interviewees repeatedly referenced the importance of the positive regard of congregational rabbis in nurturing a communal educational agency and influencing public opinion about its role in the community.

In sum, the educators interviewed largely concurred with researchers and numerous community leaders cited in previous chapters regarding the particular strengths of the St. Paul Jewish community and the numerous productive developments that resulted from its support of a central educational agency.

NOTE

1. For the full list of Planning Process Principles and Goals, see chapter 4.

Chapter 6

Current Circumstances and Future Prospects

... always start from where you really are.

—Rabbi Moshe B. Sachs, B'nai Abraham Congregation,
St. Louis Park, Minnesota, 1959–1974

Effective educational planning begins with an accurate assessment of prevalent circumstances and the options they allow. But circumstances alone cannot dictate planning. In navigating the distance between conditions and choices, educational planning also depends on a clear sense of mission. This chapter focuses on current circumstances in St. Paul, along with analysis of options available to educational planners if they choose to continue to chart its educational future in communal terms. As these circumstances come to resemble Jewish educational environments in other parts of North America, analysis of developments in St. Paul can be of value to other communities as well. With this in mind, the chapter centers on current conditions in St. Paul, but with an eye to analogous circumstances in other locales. The categories explored—*community culture*, *leadership*, *resources*, and *faculty development*—roughly correspond to those employed by Harold Himmelfarb in his paper "Jewish Education for Naught: Educating the Culturally Deprived Jewish Child." Though much has changed since the study was published in 1975, Himmelfarb's categories remain useful references points.[1]

CURRENT CIRCUMSTANCES: COMMUNITY STRUCTURE AND CULTURE

The 2004 Twin Cities Jewish Population Study estimated the Jewish population of Greater St. Paul at 10,900, approximately 2,800 of whom were between the ages of 0–17, while the 2014 Community Planning Process Findings Executive Summary Report indicated a total population of approximately 9,200.[2] In 2018, Greater St. Paul was home to two Conservative congregations and one Reform, one Humanistic, and one Chabad/Orthodox congregation. The Conservative and Reform congregations maintained congregational education programs of their own, while Chabad operated a *yeshivah* and a *cheder* that, along with the Talmud Torah, received a direct allocation from the Federation.

The community continued to employ a federation-style fundraising and allocation system that provided financial support to communal agencies (Talmud Torah, Jewish Community Center, Jewish Family Service), along with numerous other local, metropolitan, national, and international programs. Beneficiaries pursued a wide range of goals, but the Talmud Torah was the only St. Paul agency with a uniquely Jewish mission. Programs serving the larger, non-Jewish community formed a significant portion of the other two agencies' workloads and budgets.

In the preceding forty years, the prevalence of Jewish households in St. Paul's Highland Park neighborhood had been replaced by a far more diffuse residential pattern. Both of the kosher butcher shops operating in St. Paul in the 1980s and 1990s had closed, as had a kashrut-supervised restaurant, though packaged meats and other kosher-certified products were available at grocery stores and a delicatessen in the city, and the community continued to maintain a *mikveh*.

One indication of current attitudes of community members regarding educational issues was provided by the Community Planning Process's "listening sessions." According to the Executive Summary Report, the ranked proportion of all concerns mentioned by participants was:

1. Availability, Quality, and Responsiveness of Jewish Education and Social Services (24%)
2. Community Exclusivity and Unsatisfactory Outreach to Other Jews (22%)
3. Assimilation and Changes in Jewish Values, Beliefs, and Practices (20%)
4. Division and Lack of Cooperation between Jewish Organizations and Committees (13%)
5. Changes in Jewish Population Size, Attributes, and Mobility (12%)
6. High Cost of Tuition, Membership, and Services (6%)
7. Strategic, Planning, and Fundraising (4%)
8. Perceptions of Prejudice and Discrimination (1%)[3]

Though the listening sessions did not constitute a complete sample of Jewish St. Paul, the prevalence of concerns related to education, inclusion, and institutional cooperation could be taken to indicate a relatively high degree of continued support for excellent, community-based education. If so, perspectives in St. Paul would contrast sharply with American Jewish attitudes more generally, as reflected in the 2013 Pew Center study *Portrait of Jewish Americans*, which indicated that only 28 percent of respondents to the question "What does it mean to be Jewish?" chose "Being a member of a Jewish community." And, while 43 percent of respondents identified "Caring about Israel" as indicative of being Jewish, that was just one percent higher than those who chose "Having a good sense of humor."[4]

Both locally and nationally, outside of Orthodox settings, ethnic and practice-based standards of Jewish self-definition no longer predominated. In addition, for many Jews the State of Israel was now a fact (and for some, an increasingly complicated one), rather than a miracle, and the counter-cultural energy that had led back to Jewish life for many young Jews in the 1970s and 1980s was equally remote. That energy had temporarily moderated the American cultural emphasis on upward mobility, the primacy of contracted over "given" relationships, and progressive innovation over historical authenticity, but that countervailing influence was now largely spent. What remained for an increasing number of Jews, as Yeshaya Lebowitz put it, was little more than a "declared" Jewish identity.[5]

Earlier efforts to coordinate utilization of St. Paul's educational resources had been reinforced by a renaissance in Jewish education nationally, with an emphasis on the Hebrew language, classical Jewish texts, and traditional practice, in combination with a positive consensus about the role of Israel in Jewish life. These themes coincided with ideological tendencies in the Twin Cities, leading to generous investment in Jewish education by local benefactors. Resulting communal programs in both cities engaged families directly, independent of their affiliation or non-affiliation with synagogues or other organizations. However, by the end of the twentieth century, these affinities were receding, along with the bases for collaboration they offered. A decline in patronage of communal agencies generally, along with the shrinking profile of adult organizations and their youth affiliates (Young Judea, *Habonim* AZA, etc.), suggested that community members were becoming ever more accustomed to a contracting, fragmented, synagogue-centric communal structure.

Displacement of communal institutions by congregation-based programs had proven the bane of many advocates of communal education in the middle decades of the twentieth century, but the challenge was slow in coming to the Twin Cities. Well aware of what had taken place elsewhere, Dashefsky and Shapiro had asserted in their 1974 study of Jewish identity that effective Jewish education required resisting this trend, and pointed to the Talmud Torah of St. Paul as a notable exception and positive example. They maintained that unlike communal educational agencies, synagogues tend to have a constraining effect on their in-house schools. Freed of such constraints, community schools could flourish, and in doing so, strengthen the community and its constituent institutions, *including* synagogues.

More recent community planning no longer reflected an awareness that unlike churches in Christian communities, Jewish places of prayer had not functioned, historically, as the paramount communal institution, and that viewing synagogues in this way was largely the result of external influences and models. In his introduction to Hungarian rabbi Moses Weinberger's late-nineteenth-century monograph on Jewish life in New York, *Ha-Yehudim veha-Yahadut b'New York* (*The Jews and Judaism of New York*), Jonathan Sarna noted that conditions in the United States had long been conducive to this institutional shift. Weinberger's observations were colored by a deeply conservative pessimism, but his dismay at the growing preeminence of large synagogues in the face of daunting educational challenges also evidenced the conspicuousness of the changes in the eyes of a newcomer.[6]

Along with this shift, synagogues would absorb an increasing proportion of communal resources, professional and financial, resulting in a treadmill of expanded synagogue-based services, prompting increased synagogue dues and fees. Gedalyahu Alon's description of the *yeshivot* attended by the Lithuanian Jews Daniel Elazar credited with having shaped Jewish education in communities such as St. Paul is instructive in this regard. In the Lithuanian *yeshivot*, Alon observed, appointment as rabbi of a congregation was considered a secondary vocation.[7] Subsequent waves of immigrants would slow the shift in perceptions, but liberal, pluralistic environments tend to cultivate institutional equivalencies, and the "Protestantization" of synagogues would play a key role in the adaptive dynamic of American Jewish life.[8]

Seen in this light, the privileged position given communal educational agencies in the Twin Cities, rather than being the exception, had reflected the historical rule that at communal intersections, schools enjoy the right of way. A communal school was especially well situated to articulate this overarching priority, while synagogue-based programs tended to blur the distinction. By the end of the century, in the Twin Cities, as elsewhere, the blurring was becoming increasingly programmatic.

The unfolding of these developments incongruously coincided with the publication of Egon Mayer's 2003 study "Parental Perspectives on Jewish Education in the United States," which called into question the capacity of American synagogues to fulfill this role. On the basis of his research, Mayer concluded that a sizable proportion of Jewish parents were actually less likely to enroll their children in an education program associated with a synagogue. In addition, Meyer noted:

1. Cultural elements of Jewish education are likely to make it more attractive to more parents than either religious elements or secular elements.

2. Cultural elements of Jewish education are less likely to detract from the attractiveness of Jewish education even for those parents who have greater preferences for the religious elements of Jewish education or greater preferences for the more secular elements of Jewish education.[9]

Echoing Dashefsky's concerns regarding the "fractious" influence of denominational definitions, along with their growing lack of salience (over a third of Mayer's respondents found "religious" features of a curriculum inconsequential or a source of lesser attraction), Mayer observed that American Jews were increasingly uninterested in such definitions and that "the findings of this current study of parental perspectives indicate that there is a need for serious new options in Jewish education, including and especially an option of cultural, non-religious Jewish education that is outside synagogue definition."[10]

Mayer's advocacy of "secular cultural" forms of Jewish education begged for clarification of a distinction between "secular," "cultural," and "religious" at the level of the classroom. Elazar's exemplary communal agencies had rejected such distinctions as incompatible with the type of comprehensive curriculum incumbent upon a community school. That 22 percent of respondents in the Pew Center's 2013 study described themselves as "Jews of no religion," though significant, also didn't speak directly to Jewish educational goals, given the multifaceted characteristics of Jewish literatures and cultures.[11] However, Mayer's conclusion that a large proportion of Jewish parents did not see affiliation of an education program with a synagogue as a plus was a factor educational planners could ill-afford to ignore. According to the 2004 Twin Cities Jewish Community Study, roughly half of Jewish households in St. Paul were unaffiliated with a synagogue. Under such circumstances, a meaningful definition of a "communal" educational program required consideration of educational needs far beyond the confines of congregations.[12]

Susan Cobin's observations regarding the role Talmud Torah programs played in providing a point of access into the community, and as a setting for communal solidarity for families unfamiliar or uncomfortable with other ways of Jewish involvement, complemented Mayer's call for Jewish education "outside synagogue definition." That in the past, joining a synagogue had often been an *outcome* of a Talmud Torah-mediated introduction to the community, only heightened the irony of synagogue-fostered opposition to community-based educational planning and programming. Eighty years earlier, Barnett Brickner had observed:

It is impossible for the synagogue to survive if it continues to tolerate the existence of wide areas within the Jewish community where children are permitted to grow up without any Jewish education. The support of Jewish education on a community-wide basis, by the synagogue, is in the nature of self-protection and self-preservation. It is community service, not charity.[13]

The foregoing factors strongly suggested that little would be gained in a community with a communal educational agency by shifting primary responsibility for education to synagogues. The high level of concern voiced in the Planning Process listening sessions that the St. Paul community provide strong, inclusive, and collaborative educational options could be seen as corroborating this perspective, but the Educational Panel's ensuing inability to build on these considerations suggested a growing presumption, at least among some in leadership positions, that synagogues should, somehow, serve this purpose. Apprehension voiced in the listening sessions over declining Talmud Torah enrollments would be displaced in the Panel by a synagogues-first frame of reference.[14] The community's once vigorous "public self," exemplified by its agencies, now showed signs of atrophy.[15]

These developments were also manifested in day-to-day educational terms, beginning with the erosion of dedicated instructional hours. As Rabbi Morris Katz had predicted when the Talmud Torah was established, its Sunday instructional hours were eventually ceded to the synagogues for their own programs,[16] and a reduced course-load option for its high school students would follow. None of the alternative synagogue programs would restore the lost instructional hours. Successful instruction in Hebrew alone, in any form beyond rudimentary phonics, required many more hours than most St. Paul families were allotting to Jewish education, or education programs were providing. Even day schools had limited hours to meet their numerous educational objectives, and by 2017 only a small percentage of Jewish children in St. Paul were attending *any* of the Jewish day schools in the Twin Cities.

Past experience indicated that a communal approach to education could only thrive in a community-oriented environment, informed by an appreciation of the integrative potential of a community school, and its unique capacity to counter the perception that extensive Jewish learning is the exclusive domain of particular factions. In St. Paul in the 1980s and 1990s, these premises coincided with the widely held perception that the quality of instruction provided by Talmud Torah programs was comparable to what was to be expected of excellent schools generally. When joined to the particular needs of the Jewish community, this perception tended to work to the agency's advantage. More recently, however, as identification with "inherited" communities weakened and the Talmud Torah was increasingly seen as but one educational option among many, "comparable quality" more frequently worked to the institution's detriment, in keeping with a growing tendency among Americans, as highlighted in Bellah and coauthors' *Habits of the Heart*, to view such decisions primarily in purchase-of-service terms. Unlike the largely contractual community they described, the historical model of Jewish community had long been one of both descent and consent, community received *and* constructed. Future success of communal educational programs, as Cindy Reich noted, would require institutions and curricula that were deeply rooted in received culture *and* responsive to current preferences.

Moreover, genuine *communal* education could not be framed solely in terms of its appeal to more liberal-oriented constituents. If the next stage of St. Paul's story was to prove as illuminating as the one that preceded it, it required a constructive embrace of orthodox-identified community members as well. Self-chosen affinity groups are poor substitutes for a Jewish community. Based on numbers of children alone, "communal" educational planning that disregarded this division would be, at the very least, shortsighted. However, meeting this challenge would require a renewed understanding of Hillel's exhortation that though he and his companions were known as *p'rushim*/separatists/Pharisees, that was precisely what they must not become: "*Al tifrosh*/separate from the community."[17] Inspired by this vision, the rabbinic movement had affirmed the revolutionary principle that the basic community, the *minyan*, would be defined as a certain number of people, not as an aggregate of certain qualities. In contemporary Jewish communities, similarly riven by presumptions about others' incompatibility or irrelevance, maintaining such a standard continued to prove difficult.[18] Meeting this objective would involve many moving parts, the whole secured in the in-between places, where the parts engage one another. Active orthodox involvement in both the Talmud Torah of Minneapolis and St. Paul through the 1960s and 1970s bespoke a breadth of spirit among orthodox and non-orthodox Jews alike. Similarly, in the 1980s and 1990s numerous orthodox-affiliated families who lived much closer to Orthodox-affiliated Torah Academy in Minneapolis, but able to see beyond unnecessarily constrained and self-defeating definitions of "community," had chosen to send their children to the St. Paul Day School instead, drawn by its exceptional curriculum and highly regarded faculty.

Looking back on these developments, interviewee Sara Lynn Newberger commented that much now depended on reenergizing what remained of the pride St. Paul Jews took in their educational agency. In years past, the achievements of students and alumni had evidenced high standards and effective teaching, leading in turn to increased enrollments, financial support, and a rejuvenating influence on the community. The dynamic exemplified what Ellen B. Goldring characterized as reciprocally constructive educational relationships, leading to "enhanced learning . . . developing social capital . . . [and] the development and support of the entire community."[19] Though Goldring's comments specifically reference day schools, they spoke to the opportunities a multi-program agency such as the Talmud Torah afforded as well.

Prospects for revitalizing such a dynamic would depend once again, as in the past, on the support of community leaders, the focused use of resources, and the development of strong faculty and administrators.

CURRENT CIRCUMSTANCES: COMMUNITY LEADERSHIP

The decision in the 1940s to consolidate the St. Paul community's educational resources stemmed from a number of convergent factors. Among the most important of these influences was the inclination of communal leaders, from the 1940s through the 1980s, to view the long-term interests of the particular institutions with which they were associated in terms of the needs of the community as a whole. All the interviewees in chapter 5 noted the critical importance of this perspective in the most fruitful years of community-based education in St. Paul.

St. Paul's United Jewish Fund and Council had led the way in devising and resolutely pursuing a plan to focus the community's educational resources in a communal agency. The merger in the mid-1940s of St. Paul's United Jewish Fund with the Council of Jewish Social Agencies to form the *United Jewish Fund and Council* had been the product of the same forces that would subsequently move the community toward founding a communal educational agency. The growing prevalence of this perspective allowed the UJFC's first executive director, Dan Rosenberg, to claim the high ground on behalf of the community as a whole in fostering the development of robust communal agencies. The Fund and Council's efforts to consolidate educational programs in St. Paul had initially drawn a mixed response from congregational rabbis, but as the new agency grew in stature, their backing would prove among its most valuable assets. Rabbinical support for the Talmud Torah carried the unmistakable message that the best interests of the various congregations were inextricably bound up with the health of the broader Jewish community and its agencies. As recently as 2000, in response to the decision by the Temple of Aaron to establish its own supplementary program, the Fund and Council president had insisted, "The preservation of communal Jewish education remains an important value for the St. Paul Jewish community and of the United Jewish Fund and Council."[20]

A profusion of programs made no more educational or fiscal sense in 2012 than it had in the 1940s, especially in a community of St. Paul's size. In a 1983 interview, reflecting back on the drive to establish the Talmud Torah, Kokie Goldenberg, a leading figure at the Fund and Council and the Temple of Aaron in the 1940s and 1950s, placed the size of the St. Paul community at the top of a list of factors recommending a single communal educational agency.[21] However, by the time the Communal Planning Process was launched, the Federation itself, as in most other locales across the country, no longer occupied a comparable position in the community, and the support of congregational rabbis for the Talmud Torah could no longer be assumed. Faced with the increasingly precarious status of their own apparatus, it was much less likely that Federation leaders would voice opposition to congregations building separate educational programs, even when those programs were at the expense of Federation-founded and funded communal institutions.

A recounting of the Federation's evolving role in shaping Jewish education in St. Paul, notwithstanding a legacy of strong, visionary leaders, leads in turn to a deeper structural issue. The self-selecting *"tovei- ha-ir"/* "town's finest" model of decision-making has long been recognized as a problematic feature of Jewish communities ostensibly imbued with democratic values.[22] The St. Paul Planning Community Process was a promising first step toward broadening participation in communal decision-making. Organizing grassroots support for educational collaboration could help to further these values, while nurturing a deliberative infrastructure to sustain them. The continued support for communal collaboration in pursuit of excellent, affordable Jewish education voiced in the Planning Process listening sessions could be organized and energized in this way. However, such an effort could also end up further aggravating communal divisions. An overriding fear of alienating funders and exacerbating tensions between segments of the community, especially as their base of support shrank, clearly informed Federation reluctance to encourage active public involvement in their election and decision-making processes. Regarding education policy specifically, a more public process, rather than encouraging collaboration, could end up worsening rifts and further scattering resources.[23] Such risks are intrinsic to democratic practices, but loom larger when constituents don't expect such responsibilities, and are not accustomed to exercising them jointly.

Advocacy of renewed educational collaboration in the community at large also points to the need for cooperative leadership among educators themselves. The 1935 study of Jewish education in St. Paul led to the recommendation that a communal executive director of education be appointed to facilitate coordination of educational programs,[24] and one of the first steps of the Community Planning Committee of the 1940s was to channel its educational efforts through a community-wide St. Paul Bureau of Jewish Education. Similarly, the 1990 JESNA Study of the Talmud Torah recommended reestablishing a broadly empowered communal Jewish Education Committee. The reasons for coordinated use of resources in the 1940s and 1950s—"preventing duplication of effort and . . . promoting efficiency and economy of administration,"[25] "free[ing] schools of the constraints imposed by the politics, finances, and other pressures of synagogue affairs,"[26] and "offering educational guidance to the other schools functioning in the community"[27]—highlighted the need for coordinated educational leadership as well. The Community Planning Process goal that communal leaders "intentionally work together in ever-increasing collaboration and with a common purpose" reflected these same concerns. Past experience suggested that it was unlikely a truly *communal* education system could be reconstituted absent coordinated oversight. A senior educator's council, made up of highly regarded educators, could prove helpful in sustaining ongoing public discussion of educational challenges and opportunities. It could also help to organize and oversee communal workers education programs, like the program jointly sponsored by St. Paul's communal agencies in the early 1980s, and facilitate development and coordinated use of communal informational resources, including Hebrew language materials and classical texts. Each of these steps could help to heighten awareness of a "communal self," while facilitating the farsighted, efficient, and effective use of resources. Operating in cooperation with, but independent of congregations and other communal organizations, a council would be in a position to articulate and assess measurable, long-term, communal education goals, to conduct longitudinal tracking of educational outcomes, and hold constituent institutions educationally accountable to the community. Educational "success," measured simply in terms of initial enrollments and short-term student and parental "satisfaction," without reference to retention, realization of specific learning goals, and long-term attitudes and practices, has little to do with the ultimate purposes of Jewish learning. An educator's council could play a vital role in each of these areas. Potential pitfalls are evident. Such groups can succumb to factional disputes, personal grievances, or abuse of authority. However, efforts to reconcile competing programs through looser, non-administrative ad hoc committees have repeatedly proven inadequate. Such a group, provided it embodied a community's highest standards and aspirations, could help to meet fill this need.

CURRENT CIRCUMSTANCES: RESOURCES

Ultimately, fundraising is a meaningful response to a Jewish community's second most important challenge. "*How* do we pay, as parents and as a community, for renewed commitment to a communal educational institution?" logically follows the more basic question: "*Why* do we need to do this?" Only after the latter question is answered can a community conscientiously consider how to provide the financial resources necessary to meet its challenges.

St. Paul Jewish Federation 2014–2015 allocations totaled $2.45 million, with funds for the Talmud Torah making up approximately 10 percent of the total, while the 2016–2017 allocation to the Talmud Torah was approximately

20 percent lower, totaling roughly 7 percent of total allocations. By comparison, 2016–2017 allocations to the Jewish Family Service and Jewish Community Center were significantly higher than the amount allocated to the Talmud Torah, and in the case of the Community Center, well over twice the educational agency's allotment.[28]

Such a steep decline in funding cast a somber light on prospects for continued community agency based education. The collapse of the Education Panel's high school initiative, followed within days by the formation of a task force "to study education funding," further complicated the picture, with the door now open to Federation funding of disparate, congregation-based programs. In 1954, the St. Paul Bureau of Jewish Education had rejected a bid by Mount Zion to have the Bureau assume responsibility for its school on the grounds that a Reform curriculum was "educationally unsound." By contrast, past allocations to the Chabad *Cheder*, despite curricula unrepresentative of the larger Jewish community, would now serve as a precedent for funding of congregation-based programs as well.

Conversely, rebuilding a communal educational infrastructure would require *expanded* financial support, despite current low enrollments, to cover increased expenses in three areas: faculty and staff development and retention, student transportation and/or multisite programming,[29] and tuition support. What resources might be available, in St. Paul and similar communities, to meet these needs?

In Egon Mayer's 2003 study, expense was the most commonly cited "major reason" for not enrolling children in a formal Jewish education program.[30] In 2004–2006, as enrollments in its programs continued to decline, the Talmud Torah briefly experimented with a funding mechanism intended to move income from fixed tuition rates to a combination of affordable rates and voluntary contributions, but the plan proved unsustainable. The failure of the initiative highlighted a widening gap in the community between a presumed commitment to maximum accessibility, and the absence of a funding process that effectively met the resulting budgetary challenges.

The financing of public schools is instructive in this regard, as the author of the unsigned memo to the Bureau of Jewish Education Building Committee cited in Chapter 1 had observed. There is a price for the education they provide, but *communities* don't charge "tuition" for their public schools. Rather, they expect and require the backing of their educational mission by the community as a whole. Seen in this light, it is reasonable to expect financial support for Jewish communal educational programs from those who have enrolled their children, but not because they are thereby purchasing the commodity of a Jewish education for their children. In this respect, the 2004–2006 effort to reform the Talmud Torah's tuition structure was an inspired initiative, even if the particular financial configuration employed could not be maintained. But such a perspective was by no means new to St. Paul. Even in the most difficult days of the Great Depression, Louis Gordon, principal of the Jewish Educational Center School, reported to the Jewish Educational Center's membership:

> It is a simple matter for a school to balance its budget. All it has to do is to admit only children who pay full tuition fees, and employ second or third rate teachers, since the income of tuition fees will never be sufficient to employ first class teachers.
>
> I venture to say that until it will be recognized that even those who have no children in the Hebrew School are duty bound to support Jewish education, we cannot hope to make much headway with all our efforts in that direction.[31]

Gordon's observations remain pertinent nearly a century later. St. Paul still has the resources to meet this challenge, provided there emerges a renewed commitment to meeting the community's educational needs communally.

On an institutional level, this would require congregations to once again demonstrate the foresight to forego the ill-conceived "loss leader" of redundant, in-house, general Jewish educational programming. In the 1960s and 1970s, doing so had rebounded to the benefit of congregations in Minneapolis in particular, where exceptionally successful liturgical skills programs were established.[32] If a portion of resulting savings to families in the form of lower dues and fees were redirected to a communal educational program, the impact could be multiplied—provided the program proved attractive—by resulting efficiencies and the involvement and support of families not affiliated with congregations. Resources redirected in this way, along with proportional increases in Federation funding to cover associated growth in faculty and staff, could go a long way toward settling immediate financial concerns.

The often-cited Federation goal of strengthening relations between Jews around the world is directly related to the foregoing considerations. In particular, continued channeling of a large proportion of funds raised in the diaspora for development in Israel is unlikely to have much bearing on the central crisis in these relations: the dissolving of links between young Jews inside and outside of Israel. At this point in Israel's development, the task of sustaining these bonds would be far better served by using at least a portion of these funds to support excellent Jewish education in diaspora communities—education infused with Hebrew language learning and rooted in the "biblical humanist" vision, to use Martin Buber's term,[33] that had once quickened the Zionist movement and infused communal educational programs.

The political processes involved in each of the foregoing budgetary adjustments would be formidable. However, evading the critical challenge of maintaining effective local educational systems would, no doubt, solve all other future fundraising difficulties for congregations, agencies, and other beneficiaries alike, as one by one, a community's institutions pass away.

Finally, the St. Paul Talmud Torah's building and adjacent grounds constitute valuable educational resources. The site includes a spacious library, computer learning center, gymnasium, kosher kitchen, dozens of learning and gathering spaces, and a large outdoor recreation area. That Planning Process Educational Panel members would, nevertheless, repeatedly clash over the proposed high school program's location, despite the obvious advantages of employing an excellent communal educational facility, belied a serious commitment to efficient uses of community resources. The decision of Mt. Zion to offer its winter 2015 high school classes jointly with the Talmud Torah, at the Talmud Torah building, signaled a more promising perspective, but the joint program subsequently moved to Mt. Zion.[34]

A school building forms the pinnacle of sacred space in a Jewish community. Vibrant communities take due pride in the presence of such sacredness and make prudent use of the varied assets a communal educational facility may offer.

CURRENT CIRCUMSTANCES:
FACULTY DEVELOPMENT

In the course of planning for a collaborative communal high school program, the St. Paul Federation's Education Panel requested information from several high school programs around the country, in communities of a comparable size. The responses received were discouraging, both in regard to the quality of instruction offered and the skill levels of instructors. None of the programs surveyed offered a Hebrew-text core curriculum. Most required no such courses at all. All were funded at levels too low to attract and retain highly skilled instructors. By comparison, the St. Paul community's assets and options, though limited and increasingly tenuous, remain relatively strong. However, planned development of a new generation of educators, committed to communal collaboration and prepared to offer curricula that are rich in Hebrew language and classical texts, will take time, and will require, in the process, the steady support of the community.

An initiative to revitalize communal education in St. Paul would be of limited value absent skilled instructors, able to teach challenging curricula, with adequate resources and sufficient instructional hours—curricula indicative of a realistic understanding of what raising children to Jewish maturity entails. In their interviews, Dalia Vlodaver, Sara Lynn Newberger, and Rabbi Joel Gordon all emphasized the importance of opportunities Talmud Torah faculty members were given in the 1970s–1990s to grow in their learning and teaching skills. These opportunities, they agreed, were directly related to the development of an able and enthusiastic faculty.

Nurturing spiritual depth and moral acuity calls for teachers who reflect these qualities in their own lives and are skilled in helping students to articulate them in theirs. Proper development and stewardship of this resource requires ample opportunity for collaboration, strengthening of educators' skills, broadening of their Jewish learning, and encouragement of personal growth.

The process of assembling such faculties begins before teachers meet their first class, and extends beyond the classroom and school year. A first step in this direction would be to structure educational collaboration time into the work schedule of all the community's educators, along with targeted Federation funding of educator development programming. In the 1980s, regional CAJE conferences were held annually in the Twin Cities, complementing the national CAJE conferences held each summer. Both conference cycles eventually ended, leaving teachers and administrators to work in increased isolation from one another. Such circumstances undermine educators' confidence in the larger significance of their efforts, discourage collaboration, and unnecessarily complicate the sharing of resources. The value of current educational gatherings such as NewCAJE and LIMMUD[35] could be enhanced once again by associated regional events. Communal agencies are the obvious local choice for coordinating and hosting efforts of this sort.

However, it cannot be assumed that a full ensemble of requisite educators already live in a given community. In St. Paul, as elsewhere, attention needs to be given to the long-term development of a new generation of well-trained educators, committed to the local community and to a community-based model of Jewish education. Scholarships for advanced Jewish study and professional educational training would need to be part of this effort, along with increased attention to what would make a community an attractive home for Jewish educators—especially educators with the greater part of their teaching still ahead of them. The St. Paul Federation administers one such source of funds, the Milton P. and Irma C. Firestone Scholarship Fund, intended to help people preparing for Jewish community service work, and to assist staff members at Jewish agencies upgrade their skills. An energetic effort to interest potential educators in exploring the possibility, along with financial support for professional training in Jewish education, would be a logical next step in this regard. Communities have much to gain from the expansion of such opportunities. Establishing a Community Educators Development Office to seek out Jewish students at nearby colleges and universities for teaching positions and internships, especially students majoring in education and/or Jewish studies, would further advance such an effort.

Along with providing incentives to prospective new teachers, effective faculty development has long been understood to involve providing opportunities for supervised practice teaching, observation of other instructors, and experimentation with new materials and methods. These functions were among the original objectives of Samson Benderly and Mordecai Kaplan's efforts, and fostered the establishment of local Bureaus of Jewish Education,[36] though as the 1957 study of the Talmud Torah of Minneapolis noted, the Minneapolis agency was itself as well suited as a Bureau might be to provide these opportunities for its own faculty, new teachers-in-training, and other educators in the area. So, too, in St. Paul. In the 1990s, the Talmud Torah joined with Hamline University's education department to pilot a project in Jewish educational development. A full-fledged program did not follow, but it remains a highly desirable asset for replenishing the community's educational resources.

In thinking about the development of faculty, attention would also need to be given to administrative development. In St. Paul, as elsewhere, periods of greatest success for community schools correlated with school administrators who not only demonstrated administrative competency, but came to be viewed as the community's preeminent Jewish educators. The Talmud Torah's story clearly indicated that absent a highly esteemed educator in an executive position, challenges mounted. The agency has greatly benefited from the expertise of skilled and dedicated leaders who served as program directors or in other administrative positions, but the public presence of the institution as a whole has receded in the absence of an executive director who enjoyed such esteem.

In addition, maximizing the reach of St. Paul's limited resources and pool of educators requires renewed attention to Twin Cities-wide educational cooperation, in keeping with the Community Planning Process's stated goal of enhancing cooperation between the two communities. The St. Paul and Minneapolis Jewish Community Centers have recently taken significant steps in this direction, while the dissolution of the Twin Cities Jewish Middle School, precipitated by pressure to permanently locate the school in Minneapolis, proved a disheartening example of confusing cooperation with co-optation. There is much to recommend a thoughtful sharing of resources, but little to be gained from sacrificing the distinctive virtues of the St. Paul community and its institutions for the sake of "efficiency" on an intercity scale, especially given continued fragmentation educational efforts in Minneapolis.

There is also a need for regional educational outreach. Twin Cities agencies are well positioned to serve as a regional hub for educational programs in smaller communities in Minnesota and neighboring states. The lack of educational resources and well-prepared teachers has made in-depth Jewish education in such communities increasingly rare. Such an effort could include both face-to-face and distance-learning elements. Reaching outward in this way could well strengthen participating agencies in both St. Paul and Minneapolis, but care would be required to ensure, once again, that in broadening their reach, the participating institutions didn't further strain or dilute the remaining virtues of local communities on either end of the partnership.

The long-term prospects for a new generation of Jewish educators would ultimately turn on their ability to spark renewed energy and inspiration in their communities. Echoing generations of teachers before them, twentieth-century Jewish educators around the country commonly voiced dismay over their inability to speak effectively beyond the contracting lines of like-minded professionals, gathered together at ingrown conferences, or on the pages of unread journals—and yet, in St. Paul, something had gone right. Given the improbabilities inherent in their task, every generation of Jewish educators is due its share of disgruntlement, a balm against the sting that comes with the question: "If we did so well, why do things look so bad?" But a new era is beginning, and among the most valuable assets of a new generation of educators will be its capacity, though faced with renewed difficulties, to "rise with the occasion," and lift their communities in the process.

For those familiar with long-standing nation-wide efforts to revitalize Jewish education, the foregoing issues and challenges come as no surprise. Versions of the preceding recommendations appear in many studies issued in recent decades—for example, the widely referenced 1990 report *A Time to Act*, compiled by the Commission on Jewish Education in North America.[37] Its description of circumstances faced by Jewish educators around the country in the 1990s fairly matches *current* circumstances in St. Paul, if not the situation in St. Paul in the 1990s. Thirty years later, St. Paul has "caught up."

Many communities of a similar size and make-up are approaching "care-taker status"—not yet moribund, but no longer thriving; they are home to a residual communal infrastructure, but devoid of impetus. There are dozens of such middle-size locales across the country. Larger Jewish communities are typically too diffuse and disparate to articulate a stable, coherent public self, while very small Jewish communities, if they are to survive at all, find synagogue-centered organizational structures unavoidable. Communities of St. Paul's size, however, could well benefit from its example. Its story is not so idiosyncratic as to be irrelevant to the Jews of Madison, Birmingham, Tucson, or Buffalo. These cities, like St. Paul, though neighbors of larger urban centers with bigger Jewish populations, remain large and diverse enough to provide for productive intra-communal cross-fertilization, while not so institutionally profligate as to prevent effective collaboration.

There may yet be something of the Mississippi River Valley "style" Elazar so fervently lauded for St. Paul to share with other such communities. Freed of the ideological friction and institutional inertia of larger population centers, twentieth-century Midwestern Jewish communities proved fertile ground for the productive interaction of progressive and traditional forces. It is enough to observe that if the largest and most prominent American Jewish population centers of the last century had produced progressive and gifted Jewish educators, skilled communal workers, and concerned community members in equal proportion to the mid-sized communities of the Midwest, we might now be facing more positive prospects for American Jewish life as a whole.

Meeting the foregoing challenges requires effective, ongoing leadership. In communities like St. Paul, it might yet be possible to transform shortsighted "young leadership" programs into programs that introduce communal volunteers and workers to their respective positions as *sh'likhei mitzvah*—agents for fulfilling a *mitzvah*—called to assist fellow community members in discharging duties all Jews share. The primary Jewish communal agencies—those that care for the sick and elderly, provide food and shelter, provide loans and other assistance to people lacking financial resources, along with educational institutions—are all rooted in this understanding of public *agency*. Unfortunately, the term "agency," when applied to institutions, has largely come unmoored from this understanding. Restoring the link would help to clarify the integral role of such work in any individual's life as a Jew. The determination required of those responsible for sustaining the community's ethical and social infrastructure calls for nothing less. In his essay "Jewish Community as a Means and an End," Jon Levisohn comments:

> In the Jewish case, a conception of community might be developed by asking about those *mitsvot*, commandments or obligations, that apply to the community. These *mitsvot* are the exceptions, because most *mitsvot* apply to individuals. But some do not: establishing a judicial system, for example, or carrying out certain rituals, or educating children when parents are unable to do so. . . . Some communal obligations derive from or suggest a conception of community as acting *in loco parentis* (as in the case of educating children). Others derive from or suggest a conception of community as a corporate agent. . . . And others derive from or suggest the communal expression of certain deeply held values.[38]

A community school remains a most fitting cornerstone for a broader recommitment to this vision. True communities build communal institutions, communal institutions sustain communities, and community schools are the quintessential Jewish *communal* institution. If Dashefsky is correct that "communal Jewish education, as opposed to congregational education, placed the focus on education" and that, therefore, "there is a need for *consolidation of religious schools to create regional Jewish educational centers*"; if he is right to maintain that such an approach can indeed "free schools of the constraints imposed by the politics, finances, and other pressures of synagogue affairs," then the formation, or reformation of communal educational agencies can be a crucial step toward revitalization in communities like St. Paul. However, a communal institution must begin with, and ever return to genuine communal common ground. "Community school" as a stand-in for "denominationally unaligned" is not enough. Without a community—not simply an affinity group, a constituency, or a "market share"—"community school" is a misnomer. As has been noted, many of a community's strengths may well stem from the givens of circumstance—demographic, geographic, and ideological. In the Twin Cities, the Mississippi River proved one such circumstance, helping to define the St. Paul community in physical and social terms favorable to a stronger sense of community and the development of communal institutions. Progressive civic leadership in St. Paul was another such "given." Educational planners in other locations, facing less favorable circumstances—larger or smaller populations, more diffuse housing patterns, sharper internal ideological and experiential divides, more severe external pressures—are left with the daunting challenge of constructing functional equivalents. Larger economic or social forces can undercut the best of efforts, as occurred in other Midwest locales such as Duluth-Superior and Fargo, to the north. However, there is no indication that such circumstances are imminent in St. Paul. On the contrary, as the twenty-first century progresses, economic and social conditions are as promising in the Twin Cities as anywhere in the United States. After fifty years of decline, the population of St. Paul is once again approaching the size it reached in the 1960s, and the city has been the recent recipient of numerous awards and top rankings in a number of areas related to economic health and quality of life.[39]

NOTE ON THE DEFINITION OF "COMMUNITY SCHOOL"

It has become common for "independent" private Jewish schools that are unaligned with a particular movement to be termed "community schools." Congregation-based educational alliances are also commonly construed as "communal programs."[40] However, such programs signal a very different perspective than the sensibility that informed the development of communal agencies such as the Talmud Torah of St. Paul. The European communal Talmud Torah, the *heder m'tukan* movement, and the American communal agency model, all drew inspiration from rabbinic resistance to the privatization of Jewish education. In various times and places private tutors have been engaged to teach the children of those who can afford them, but already in early rabbinic sources the description of "*batei rabban*" indicate a much broader constituency. These sources cast teachers as agents of the community, commissioned to assist parents in fulfilling the *mitzvah* to teach one's children, and thus entitled, for example, to zoning variances for their classes.[41] In European communities the title "Talmud Torah" came to be linked specifically with institutions established to meet this communal responsibility. The communal agency model stemmed from this same premise.

Hebrew language charter schools also imply a very different orientation. In accessing the resources of the broader public to further an educational goal of particular interest to Jews—a problematic policy, pursued at the price of isolating Hebrew language learning from the broader spectrum of Jewish educational goals—such programs also signal abdication of Jewish public responsibility. Though the resources employed are "public" in a broader sense, the effect, vis-à-vis a *Jewish* "public self," is similarly privatizing. As the website of a charter school in a Minneapolis suburb that features Hebrew language instruction asserts, "Because of our small teacher-to-student ratios, academic rigor, uniforms, and strong parent involvement, our public school feels more like a private academy."[42]

A communal school cannot produce a multigenerational, Jewishly knowledgeable and concerned community out of whole cloth. As Geoffrey Bock commented at the close of his 1975 paper "Does Jewish Education Matter?," "American Jewry must ultimately contend with the social context of Jewish education. 'Better' Jewish education can hardly replace a dynamic Jewish community."[43] However, unlike a congregation-based program, charter school, or private school, a communal school has the potential, increasingly rare amid fractious and privatizing forces, to substantiate and extend a community's inclusive, public dimensions.

NOTES

1. The long-term relevance of Himmelfarb's research, along with Bock's related study, has been challenged, both in terms of its initial limitations, and changing circumstances. For a summary of the criticism, and analysis of the research using updated data, see M. Boxer, "Revisiting 'The Non-Linear Impact of Schooling': A First Step toward a Necessary Corrective," in *Sociological Papers Formal and Informal Jewish Education: Lessons and Challenges in Israel and in the Diaspora*, Vol. 17 (Sociological Institute for Community Studies, Bar-Ilan University, 2012–13).

2. Sheskin, *2004 Twin Cities Jewish Community Study*, 3–3, 5–23. Jewish Federation of St. Paul Community Planning Process Findings, Executive Summary, March 4, 2014, Appendix II.

3. Planning Process findings Executive Summary, March 4, 2014, 14–15.

4. "A Portrait of Jewish Americans." http://www.pewforum.org/2013/10/01/jewish-american-beliefs-attitudes-culture-survey/.

5. Yeshayahu Leibowitz, *Emunah, Historiah, v'Arakhim* (Jerusalem: Academon, 2002), 208. Ironically, the protean nature of the *"Clal Yisrael"* construct would come

to be identified by some as contributing to the dissolution of Jewish affinities. Krasner notes that already in the 1960s doubts about the model were being voiced not only in Orthodox circles, but also from leading figures in the Conservative movement. Both St. Paul and Minneapolis Talmud Torah curricula would remain rooted in classical Jewish sources and the Hebrew language, and aligned with traditional Jewish practice, through the end of the century, but the paradigm was clearly susceptible to less substantive applications. See Krasner, *The Benderly Boys and American Jewish Education*, 325–26.

6. Jonathan Sarna, *People Walk on Their Heads: Moses Weinberger's Jews and Judaism in New York* (New York: Holmes and Meier, 1982), 7–15. Weinberger's closing footnote references the anecdote in the Jerusalem Talmud, *Shekalim* 5:4, in which R. Hama bar Hanina remarks to R. Hoshaya, while walking among the synagogues of Lod, "How much money my ancestors sank into all this!" to which Hoshaya replies, "How many *souls* your ancestors sank here. . . . Weren't there people engaged with Torah [who could have used that money]?!"

7. See Gedalyahu Alon, "The Lithuanian Yeshivas," in *The Jewish Expression*, Judah Goldin, ed. (New York: Bantam, 1970).

8. On the early stages of this process see Marcus, *United States Jewry, 1776–1985*, chapter 7, and Lance J. Sussman, "Isaac Leeser and the Protestantization of American Judaism," *American Jewish Archives*, 38 (1986): 5–6. Gershom Scholem would argue that a related "drive to imitate" led to the emergence of the "Star/Shield of David" as the preeminent Jewish symbol. See Gershom Scholem, *The Messianic Idea in Judaism, and Other Essays in Jewish Spirituality* (New York: Schocken, 1971), 257–81.

9. Egon Mayer, *Parental Perspectives on Jewish Education in the United States* (New York: Center for Cultural Judaism, 2005), 35.

10. Mayer, *Parental Perspectives on Jewish Education in the United States*, 6.

11. "A Portrait of Jewish Americans," 7.

12. Fifty-six percent of respondents indicated that they were synagogue members. The study also noted that St. Paul had a relatively high percentage of respondents who identified themselves as "Just Jewish." Sheskin, *2004 Twin Cities Jewish Community Study*, 15, 22.

13. Brickner, "Communal Responsibility of the Synagogue to the Jewish School," 147.

14. Jewish Federation of St. Paul Community Planning Process Findings, Executive Summary, 11–14.

15. In the summer of 2016 a St. Paul Jewish Community Center staff person told a Talmud Torah volunteer who had asked to post a flyer announcing an event related to the school's sixtieth anniversary that the Center no longer had a community bulletin board, as it was a kind of private community center, with members.

16. Into the 1980s the afternoon program continued to provide sparsely attended Sunday morning classes for elementary age students not participating in synagogue programs. Harold Smith, president of the Talmud Torah from 1967 to 1970, comments on these changes in his memoir *My Life: The First 95 Years*, 103.

17. Mishnah, *Avot* 2:5.

18. This insight appears to inform A. I. Kook's understanding of the significance of the *minyan* and his inclusive understanding of the Jewish community. See comments on עת רצון in: A. I. Kook, *Olat Ra'yah* (Jerusalem: Mossad ha-Rav Kook, 1983), 261.

19. E. B. Goldring, "Building Community Within and Around Schools: Can Jewish Day Schools Measure Up?" in *Jewish Day Schools and Jewish Communities*, A. Pomson and H. Deitcher, eds. (Oxford: Littman, 2009), 33.

20. Hoffman, "Temple of Aaron School Decision Riles St. Paul Jews," 1.

21. United Jewish Fund and Council Oral History Project, Kalman (Kokie) Goldenberg interview, August 29, 1983. http://reflections.mndigital.org/cdm/compoundobject/collection/jhs/id/836/rec/152.

22. Observers have long noted this glaring disjunct in American Jewish communal life. See, for example, Benjamin M. Kahn's chapter on "Leadership in the Jewish Community," in *Tradition and Contemporary Experience*, A. Jospe, ed. (New York: Schocken, 1970), 348–58.

23. In 1999 the author published an editorial in the American Jewish World calling for greater democratization of communal processes, prompting a request from a former president of the St. Paul Fund and Council to speak with the author about the piece. In the ensuing conversation the former president offered a particularly pointed argument against such reforms: The author's "beloved Talmud Torah" would certainly suffer at the hands of the St. Paul community at large.

24. Chiat and Proshan, *We Rolled Up Our Sleeves*, 78–79.

25. *American Jewish World*, January 13, 1956, 1.

26. Dashefsky and Shapiro, *Ethnic Identification among American Jews*, 124.

27. Ruffman, *Survey of Jewish Education in Minneapolis*, 56.

28. Jewish Federation of St. Paul website. http://jewishstpaul.org/who-we-are/financials.

29. Given a more diffuse Jewish residential pattern in St. Paul in recent years, reestablishing a bus system, and/or multiple sites, would likely boost enrollment in a communal program, though a multisite program would undercut the socially integrating function of a central agency. "Circuit-riding" faculty and regular interbranch events could mitigate this effect, while contributing to curricular consistency.

30. Mayer, *Parental Perspectives on Jewish Education in the United States*, 28. However, he also notes that expense was offered as a major reason for not enrolling children in an education program by fewer than a third of all respondents.

31. Principal's Report, Annual Meeting of the Jewish Education Center Association, May 24, 1932. Talmud Torah of St. Paul Archives.

32. A number of prominent Hebraists and liturgical experts are dual alumni of the Talmud Torah of Minneapolis and a concurrent synagogue skills program, including Miles Cohen (JTS), Noam Zion (Hartman Institute), Perry Rank (Rabbinical Assembly), and Jay Frailich (HUC).

33. Regarding Buber's own use of the term and associated educational implications, see *"Humaniut Mikra-it,"* in *Darko shel Mikra*, Martin Buber, ed. (Jerusalem: Mossad Bialik, 1978), 36–40.

34. The collaboration has continued, with class sessions held at Mt. Zion.

35. LIMMUD, an international Jewish educational foundation, was founded in the United Kingdom in 1990. It is best known for its educational conferences. NewCAJE was founded in 2010.

36. Krasner, *Benderly Boys*, 55–58.

37. *A Time to Act (עת לעשות): The Report of the Commission on Jewish Education in North America* (Lanham, MD: University Press of America, 1990).

38. Alex Pomson and Howard Deitcher, *Jewish Day Schools, Jewish Communities* (Oxford: Littman, 2009), 104.

39. See http://www.stpaul.gov/index.aspx?NID=4639, and http://www.startribune .com/a-growing-st-paul-gets-hip-to-millennials-and-retirees-alike/304828641/.

40. See Krasner, *Benderly Boys*, Part III ("Between *K'lal Yisrael* and Denominationalism, 1940–1965"), regarding the trend toward educational alliances.

41. Baba Batra 20b–21a. A broader constituency is apparent from zoning regulations, locations, descriptions of attendees (e.g., fatherless children), and the fact that the students were taught in groups. If in this regard the Talmud's description of actions attributed to Y'hoshua ben Gam'la are idealized, they nevertheless reflect prevailing rabbinic values.

42. https://www.agamim.org/. Accessed August 20, 2017.

43. Bock, *Does Jewish Education Matter?* 10.

Chapter 7

The Arc and the Ark

A hundred years have passed since Philip Kleinman and niece Anna arrived in St. Paul; eighty years since the report on Jewish education in St. Paul recommended the appointment of an executive director of education for the community; over sixty years since the opening of the Talmud Torah of St. Paul and the dedication of its new home on Mississippi River Boulevard; forty years since the JESNA report that included the recommendation that a Jewish day school in St. Paul be considered, and which led to the hiring of Rabbi Joel Gordon as executive director of the Talmud Torah; twenty years since peak enrollments in the Day School, and the opening of the Twin Cities Jewish Middle School; a hundred years in the unlikely educational history of a Jewish community, in a Midwestern river town, on the upper Mississippi.

In 2016, planning for a sixtieth Talmud Torah anniversary celebration occasioned mixed emotions from community members who saw only a minor distinction between colloquial use of "Talmud Torah" to describe earlier St. Paul afternoon schools, and the founding of the Talmud Torah of St. Paul as a unified communal agency. Compounding the confusion, a visitor to the Talmud Torah of St. Paul's first home no longer finds any indication of the building's original function. It is now the property of the Temple of Aaron and is currently occupied by a private Montessori school. The dedicatory plaque identifying the facility as the George Kaplan Educational Building is gone, as are all other indications of the building's history.[1] No trace remains of the decades-long effort to establish a central Jewish educational agency in St. Paul, culminating in the construction of the building, nor of the educators, staff and students who worked and learned there. Come upon the building now and one finds *g'veret aheret b'otah ha-simlah*: A different lady in the same dress. No visible vestige remains of the moment, as Janet Kroll described it in her coverage of the cornerstone ceremony in June of 1956, when, "dipping the trowel in cement, Mrs. Greenberg and Mr. Kaplan stood silently a moment—the two people most responsible for bringing into reality a vision of cultural achievement and contribution to the American way of life on the shores of the Mississippi, in St. Paul."[2]

It was a time of growing resources and confidence. A historical respite, when "cultural achievement" and "the American way of life" were a comfortable match for the Jews of St. Paul. They had made it across to a relatively secure place and time, not yet encumbered by the renewed apprehensions of twenty-first-century Jewish communities.

The visible signs and shared sensibilities associated with those places and events have faded. But what remains, at a deeper level? What would the *current* St. Paul community look like if educators in the 1920s and 1930s, and community leaders in the 1940s and 1950s, had not initiated the events described in the preceding chapters? What if a central communal education agency had never been established? Alternative histories must be approached with caution, but some probabilities are clear enough.

First, there are the people who were drawn to St. Paul to teach and learn. Educational collaboration brought several generations of gifted teachers and administrators to the city. Those who came earlier helped to attract and retain later arrivals, and their influence extended well beyond the confines of the specific programs in which they were employed. The ability to retain these staff members, who often came with families who would also serve the community, depended on providing sufficient hours and adequate salaries, suitable facilities, ongoing opportunities for continued professional development, and co-workers with whom they could learn and collaborate. Being able to meet these needs was greatly facilitated by bringing the community's most able Jewish educators together in a single, multi-school communal agency.

Talmud Torah faculty members, administrators, and families were, in turn, actively involved in forming Beth Jacob Congregation, which quickly rose to national prominence.[3] Ruth Gavish, principal of the Supplementary School and the first director of the Day School, referring in particular to the founding of Beth Jacob, observed, "Of course, the Day School wasn't the only cause for the changes, but it provided the energy, the stimulus and the push. One mustn't underestimate the influence of children, especially when they come home filled with enthusiasm and excitement."[4]

The proximity of the Talmud Torah to the Temple of Aaron from 1956 through 1996 undoubtedly benefited that congregation as well, enhancing its profile and appeal. The agency's subsequent move to the Hamline Avenue site, along with the founding of Beth Jacob and the retirement of Bernard Raskas, disrupted this relationship.[5] The latter half of the 1990s was punctuated by unsuccessful attempts to reach new terms for cooperation between the congregation and agency, but prior to these developments the connection had generally been seen as mutually beneficial.

It is fair to assume that the impact of community-wide educational collaboration on the other St. Paul congregations and communal agencies was also positive, if less pronounced. Enrollment in Talmud Torah programs often served as an entry point for further involvement in community programs for youth (e.g., camping) and adults (e.g., The Melton Mini-School, initially hosted by the St. Paul Jewish Community Center, now affiliated with the St. Paul Talmud Torah), as well as synagogue affiliation. One striking indication of the broad range of congregational rabbinic support the institution enjoyed through the first years of this century was the enrollment in the St. Paul Day School of children of rabbis from all of the Twin Cities Conservative congregations, the grandchildren of two conservative congregational rabbis, and the children of three of the last four senior rabbis at Mt. Zion.

Schools can also help to hone and focus a community's ethical energies.[6] Once again, caution is in order. How to gauge the cumulative effects of countless conversations between parents and children about classroom dilemma discussions and Justice Committee cases, or between parents and Talmud Torah faculty? Nevertheless, there is reason to believe that here too the school's influence extended well beyond its classrooms.[7]

In addition, establishing and maintaining a shared educational agency undoubtedly had an integrative effect on the community's members and institutions. As the American Jewish World observed in 1948 regarding the formation of the committee to "formulate a unified plan for Jewish education in St. Paul" (hauntingly similar to the mission of the St. Paul Education Planning Panel nearly seventy years later), the Talmud Torah of Minneapolis had already demonstrated how a central educational agency could prove not only an educational asset, but "a community blessing."[8] Subsequent frictions, frustrations, and disappointments notwithstanding, centrifugal, disintegrative forces in the community would have likely proven even stronger.

Ultimately, a fully *communal* educational institution would also include the active involvement of Chabad-affiliated families, and this goal is yet to be realized. Nevertheless, the Chabad community, though largely autonomous in educational terms, also benefited from the Talmud Torah's influence. Over and above programs that brought students to the local Chabad House, and Chabad-sponsored "how-to" presentations at the Talmud Torah, intracommunal relations were enhanced by the positive regard the Talmud Torah, along with the other communal agencies, strove to maintain toward all sectors of the community. The level of learning of Talmud Torah faculty, along with the depth of its curricula and commitment to halakhic standards in its daily operations, made for less contested, if not yet more common, ground.

In gauging the Talmud Torah's continued influence, it also can be noted that alumni and their families continue to figure prominently in communal affairs. Graduates now serve as Federation committee members, communal officers, and agency heads. Three of the six St. Paul Talmud Torah students to become rabbis have returned to live and work in the community. The current directors of the local Hillel Foundation and the St. Paul Jewish Community Center are also alumni, as was the first director of Minneapolis's *Yachad* program.

The St. Paul Jewish community of the 1950s–1990s was no Camelot, any more than Jewish Minneapolis had been at mid-century, though it is often characterized as the Minneapolis community's "golden age." Both communities remained a familiar mix of right and wrong, moral courage and failing, among the prominent and *prost* alike. And in both communities far too many children came away from their first encounter with Jewish education with lasting memories of frustration and boredom, of hurtful classmates, or instructors. Nevertheless, there is ample reason to conclude that by and large, a communal, agency-based approach to Jewish education exerted a very positive influence on both communities, and it was an important factor in sustaining a sense of communal integrity and purpose.[9]

But what, then, if the arc of communal Jewish education in St. Paul were to continue to slope downward? What if the socially integrative dynamic and the range and quality of instruction associated with the Talmud Torah in the latter half of the twentieth century were no longer a part of Jewish life in St. Paul?

The question can be approached, first of all, geographically. Sixty years ago, the logic of geographically defined "local" Jewish communities was presumed—communities small enough in numbers and area to be undergirded by a high degree of personal and familial bonds, but large enough to sustain an effective institutional infrastructure; familiar enough to cultivate a strong sense of belonging, while large enough to allow for unexpected encounters and new relationships; communities of physical proximity, yet diverse enough to require their members, as with a *minyan*, to count the "present, unchosen Other." Learning to *make* a community of Jews who happen to find themselves in the same place was once a primary characteristic of the collective Jewish experience. The Talmud Torah was a signal example of this process in action.

If a geographic coordinate of community were retained, but "local" now referred not to the 10,000 Jews of greater St. Paul, but the 40,000 Jewish residents of the Twin Cities, the alteration of scale in population and area would present its own problems, along with those posed by contrasting community histories and recent collaborative failures. Distances alone would pose challenges. In the 1960s, most of St. Paul's Jewish households were clustered within the four-square miles of the Highland Park neighborhood, and in the 1980s, within a ten-mile radius. By comparison, a combined St.

Paul-Minneapolis Jewish Community would extend fifteen to twenty-five miles on either side of the Mississippi River. Diffusion of households and institutions on this scale, with the ensuing loss of everyday familiarity—a loss of "common ground" in its most basic sense—would make consolidation of Twin Cities communal institutions quite a different matter than the prevention of "duplication of effort" and promotion of "efficiency and economy of administration" sought by the United Jewish Fund and Council in the 1950s. Under these circumstances, Jewish St. Paul would likely soon come to resemble an appendage of the larger Minneapolis community; its vestigial features the lingering smile of a communal Cheshire cat.

But accelerated geographic diffusion is at once both a cause and effect of a larger disintegrative process. Recent research on trends in affiliation, personal practice, and attachment to the Jewish People indicate that a growing proportion of those who continue to identify themselves as American Jews (let alone those with no more than residual Jewish connections) are largely uninterested in rooting that identity, even in the most contingent ways, in *any* Jewish community, local or otherwise.[10] Physical characteristics of the local community had once meshed with the widely held assumption that there was a substantive core to Jewish life, rooted in personal relationships and common practices—an evident cultural legacy, and a shared future that pointed to Jewish education rooted in Hebrew, the Tanakh, and classical rabbinic literature.[11] In the 1940s and 1950s, Jewish educational reorganization in St. Paul was buoyed by widespread support for institutional and pedagogical reforms, but these changes, though modernizing in regard to classroom atmosphere and technique, remained relatively traditional in content. Community was still linked, to a great extent, to such "givens."

Talmud Torah administrators and teachers strained to maintain a fully egalitarian curriculum, centered on the Hebrew language, moral and aesthetic awareness, classical Jewish texts, and *mitsvot*, but by the late 1990s, outside of Orthodox settings, the priority traditionally placed on a text-based Jewish education in original languages was in broad decline. Reports accumulated indicating declining interest in substantive Jewish curricula throughout the country. The Pew Study would be followed by the Jewish Education Project's *Generation Now* Report, which explicitly deemphasized acquisition of "Jewish knowledge" as an educational goal for Jewish teenagers, with neither "Torah" or "Hebrew" mentioned in its fourteen "Outcomes."[12] Educators now faced the perplexing challenge of providing a Jewish education no longer focused on things distinctly Jewish. Alternative slogans and programs bloomed and withered, all struggling with the accumulating evidence that *Torah* and *mitsvot* were no longer enough to meet the challenges and opportunities of life in modern liberal societies, and ever more acutely, not enough to retain the interest and loyalties of Jewish youth.[13]

And so, one more consequence, intended or not, of continued thinning of the communal fabric: inadvertent validation of the claim that *talmud torah*, rooted in classical sources, no longer constituted common ground, but was rightly the domain of Orthodox Jews alone.

And if the "generation now" of Jewish students comes with far different expectations, there is a generational crisis among educators as well. The conundrums that come with conveying so deep and broad a legacy in ways that resonate with contemporary expectations are compounded by the challenge of finding faculty able to thread so fine a pedagogical needle, day by day. The efforts of Phillip Kleinman, Anna Kleinman Schwartz, Louis Gordon, Albert Elazar and other community-oriented educators gradually transformed the St. Paul community's profile. Their vision would profoundly shape the community, and in doing so, draw other talented educators in their wake. But a century has now passed since the Kleinmans arrived in St. Paul. Talmud Torah programs have continued to employ highly trained faculty members, but staff members who came to the school during its ascendant years and contributed to the vitality of the community as a whole are approaching retirement, or have retired already. The agency has also benefited from able and devoted volunteer administrative support, but many of these volunteers are, likewise, reaching retirement and continued dependence on such assistance only highlights the institution's accumulating difficulties.

And yet, some community members have come to believe, as did supporters of the Hebrew Institute in the 1950s, that renewed efforts to reintegrate current educational programs will inevitably shortchange some segments of the community, to the advantage of others. The view that the Talmud Torah of St. Paul was as successful as it was because it was a *communal* institution, continues to be broadly shared, but it isn't unanimous.

One such observer of developments in St. Paul, a life-long member of the community and an active participant in communal affairs, is representative of the latter perspective. Interviewed in June 2015, this community member contended that the administrative and financial link between the Day School and Supplementary School, far from facilitating greater "economy of scale" and mutually beneficial collaboration, ultimately destabilized both schools, while needlessly antagonizing supplementary school families. The community member concluded that the founding of the Day School undermined the United Jewish Fund and Council's original objective for the Talmud Torah of "preventing duplication of effort and . . . promoting efficiency and economy of administration" and that even with unsustainably low Day School tuition, leading to ever increasing allocations from the Federation, the Talmud Torah ended up "telling a great story for a limited number of kids," while clinging to the self-image of a "community" institution. Dissatisfaction with the arrangement, the observer concluded, catalyzed support at the Temple of Aaron for a supplementary program of its own, while the absence of an institutional link between the Minneapolis Talmud Torah and Minneapolis Day School had worked to the benefit of both institutions.[14]

A particularly troubling aspect of the critic's analysis is the assertion that a communal agency ought not be home to both a day school and supplementary program. That the Talmud Torah had been the home of multiple schools was exceptional, to be sure. Quite possibly, no other American Jewish educational agency attempted a comparable range of programs. The effort was so unusual as to lead no less an observer than Daniel Elazar to view the St. Paul Talmud Torah and St. Paul Day School as competing institutions.[15] If the observer's analysis is flawed, it is clear that the perception that the founding of the Day School was an implicit deprecation of the supplementary program, and of those who continued to choose it, has taken its toll. The Community Planning Process Education Panel's inability to affirm any educational common ground suggests the growing prevalence of the critic's perspective, despite the evident advantages resulting from the integration of budgets, personnel, and curricula among the agency's schools.

Some community members now find the very name "St. Paul Talmud Torah" irksome.[16] In the eyes of many, it is no longer the "dream of decades" American Jewish World reporter Janet Kroll envisaged at the laying of the cornerstone for its new home overlooking the Mississippi. And yet, its continued, if fitful, presence suggests that at least some community members are still dreaming that dream. If, however, it were to close, or accede to a radically attenuated mission, there is scant reason to believe this sort of education would soon return, and in light of the foregoing observations, the loss would be fivefold: (1) Further erosion of crucial links to diverse Jewish communities worldwide, including the Hebrew-speaking Jews of Israel. (2) The dependence of the community on the willingness of knowledgeable and able, communally-oriented teachers to make their home in St. Paul, despite waning educational resources for themselves and their families. (3) The accelerated evaporation of a "common language of Jewish life"—metaphorically, culturally, and linguistically. (4) The loss of the community's only institution dedicated to providing a wide range of Jewish educational opportunities to all community members, affiliated or unaffiliated, of all ages and ideological inclinations, beyond rudiments that are all too quickly outgrown, forgotten, or spurned. (5) The displacement of Jewish learning from the center, to the periphery of communal purposes, and the resulting loss of communal common ground.

Torah, though a project of a hundred generations and a thousand locations, can only be realized in the here-and-nows of lived educational relationships. But if misgivings about the possibility of renewed collaboration prove so extensive as to preclude the Jews of St. Paul, *as a community*, from even attempting to meet the educational challenges they face, it can only be concluded that a significant proportion of the population no longer see themselves as participants in the *"public* self" the Talmud Torah long represented. If so, it remains to be seen how much longer before references to "the St. Paul Jewish community" will be confined to learned footnotes about communities that once were. The concerted effort leading to its founding in 1956 began a decade earlier with the forming of a "Community Planning Committee." The charge given the Community Planning Process Education Panel in 2015 was strikingly similar to that of their predecessors: Focus on community-wide issues from a community-oriented perspective. Much would hinge on how the panel and subsequent communal bodies understood this charge.

Rabbi Joel Gordon concluded his 1988 article "The Talmud Torah of St. Paul: A Picture of a Community School" with a brief reflection on the question "Is the Talmud Torah Experience a Model?":

> Many of the reasons for the Talmud Torah's survival and its successes must be attributed to good fortune, divine providence or benign neglect. Others are indications of a communal spirit and an understanding of and respect for individual differences which have brought the oft-competing forces to work together. Today this kind of system may be considered an alternative. The future will tell us if communal education must become a necessity for many American Jewish communities.[17]

Thirty years later, that telling future has arrived.

However, in the meantime, the ebbing of educational collaboration in St. Paul threatens to preempt the relevance of its story for other locales. Its experience is of limited value to other Jewish communities if the Jews of St. Paul cannot recommit to a collaborative future. Time will tell whether a highly productive mix of circumstances and choices not only led to short-term advances in the past, but that those gains were conserved and extended in the face of subsequent challenges; that the arc of covenantal commitments made then, will continue to trace the community's reach and aspirations. Stories of episodic success may be interesting and they may even prove inspiring, but that alone is no proof that they are of lasting significance. That proof will take more time, and in the meantime, the steady support of community members. With that support, St. Paul may yet experience renewed communal vigor. If so, its example can point the way to a more hopeful future for other communities as well. Ultimately, Jewish communities, *as* Jewish communities, have only lives of Torah to offer the greater human project, and the way to Torah is *talmud torah*.

The story of Jewish education in St. Paul may also be of interest to non-Jewish communities, similarly rooted in a weave of language, culture, and kinship. Alongside the bend in the Mississippi Janet Kroll once likened to the banks of the Jordan and the rivers of Babylon, other communities now cluster. They, along with Anishinabe and Dakotah people, the people for whom Gideon Pond composed his Hebrew-Dakotah Dictionary, and who would suffer exile as Jews were first settling along the river's lofty bluffs, are confronted by challenges similar to those Jews have faced. They, and others, may find something of value in the St. Paul Jewish community's story; its efforts to keep faith with its heritage, while grappling with the opportunities and challenges that come with living in a diverse and, in principle, pluralistic society. Their educators may find something useful in the blend of traditional sources, contemporary educational methods, and progressive values characteristic of the Talmud Torah's programs in the last quarter of the twentieth century—something inspirational in the ways the community responded to the testing of the "givens" of Jewish life that came with liberalization. It is, all told, an *arcing* narrative of partial success and ample failures, the product of a particular time and place. As such, it could be seen as of limited relevance to others. Its value, however, isn't as a source of formulas for success, but as a record of educational intersections of the timely and timeless in the life of a community just around the bend.

Rabbi Bernard Raskas would relate that for the discerning, the river itself conveyed such lessons, tracing the roots of a celebrated interfaith metaphor to the Ford Bridge, between St. Paul and Minneapolis. Raskas recalled that in the spring of 1964, as he and Abraham Joshua Heschel were walking across the bridge, they paused to contemplate the Mississippi as it flowed around a small island just to the south. Raskas remembered Heschel responding to the scene with the comment, "No religion is an island," and then immediately setting to work on what would become his address "No Religion Is an Island" at Union Theological Seminary in Manhattan the following year. A memorable message, born on the Mississippi, and delivered on the Hudson.[18]

The educational objectives and outcomes chronicled in the preceding pages cannot be fully evaluated in months or years, but in generations. The gains the St. Paul Jewish community harvested at the end of the twentieth century grew from seeds that were sown and tended by people who had by then passed on, or were among the graying. Those who would now continue the work must likewise be prepared to build for a future that extends over bridges they may never cross. If there is a single consistent feature of biblical portrayals of Israel's founders and shepherds, it is that the most important work of a generation is never finished in that generation; sometimes the task requires more time, sometimes different times. Sometimes next steps await generations not bound by the experiences and memories that defined the generation that preceded them.[19] A generation inevitably comes to the banks of its Jordan, while the ark, and the arc, move on:

How much more praise deserv'd thy beauty's use,
If thou could'st answer—"This fair child of mine
Shall sum my count, and make my old excuse—"
Proving by his beauty by succession thine.
　　This were to be new-made when thou art old,
　　And see thy blood warm when thou feel'st it cold.[20]

Sixty years is a short time when measured against the sweep of Jewish history, and a century is little more than a prologue. Time will tell. Somewhere in the walls of the previous home of the Talmud Torah of St. Paul on Mississippi River Boulevard there remains a time capsule, placed there in 1956 as part of the cornerstone ceremony, and left behind when the agency moved to its new home on Hamline Avenue. As reporter Janet Kroll observed:

> Following the "Shehehiyonu" (prayer of Thanksgiving) by Rabbi Morris C. Katz, Mr. Rosenthal placed a steel box on the platform and called upon the heads of the various organizations connected with the Talmud Torah to deposit their membership lists and other data on their activities. Louis Gordon, Talmud Torah principal, did it for the T.T. faculty and staff; Miryom Arnold, for the student council; Victor Toushin, for the members of the building committee; Mrs. Max Arnold, for the P.T.A.; Mrs. Marcus Hertz, for the pre-school mothers; Irwine E. Gordon, Talmud Torah president, for the board of directors; and Charles Harris, responsible for the architecture of the building, inserted some blueprints.
>
> 　Mr. and Mrs. George Kaplan were given the signal honor of inserting a memorandum of their gift of $100,000, pledged in 1949 and addressed to posterity.[21]

The steel box placed in the Talmud Torah's wall that day remains there, an improbable descendant of the long-forgotten scroll discovered in the Temple in the days of King Josiah.[22] If the box were recovered, and the record of hopes and expectations placed in it were read aloud once again by the posterity the Kaplans addressed, who knows what embers might be stirred, but this much is certain: אבן מאסו הבונים היתה לראש פנה—the stone now neglected was once the cornerstone of a provident and vibrant community.

The day is short and the tasks have multiplied. A shrinking and graying community may well lose track of the hard lessons learned from educational collaboration. If so, the perseverating apprehension that neglect of learning foreshadows social disintegration may be borne out in St. Paul, as it has been elsewhere. Alternatively, the community, while still a community, may yet muster its resources, focus its efforts, and move decisively to apply those lessons in pursuit of a viable future. However, this will require recognition of the urgency of the situation, *and* recommitment to long-term planning, overarching commonalities, and persistent effort. Given this awareness and these commitments, the St. Paul Jewish community might once again provide a "highly illuminating" demonstration of the power of common ground.

Something in St. Paul might once again go right—another little miracle on the upper Mississippi. Despite disappointment and reversal, Kim Marsh's vision remains prescient: "How do we assure creative Jewish continuity? I believe that the linchpin is in the provision of quality Jewish education *for ourselves and for our children and grandchildren.*"

NOTES

1. After the move to the building on Hamline Ave, the plaque could be glimpsed for a time behind a chair in the library, beneath a photo of Louis Gordon. It has since been placed in storage. The agency's afternoon school and Midrasha continue to bear Kaplan's name.

2. Janet Kroll, "People of Vision See Dream Fulfilled At. St. Paul T. T. Corner-Stone Laying," *American Jewish World*, June 22, 1956, 15.

3. The congregation would be featured in the 2000 study *Jews in the Center: Conservative Synagogues and Their Members*, and included in the 2009 *Newsweek* list of the "25 Most Vibrant Jewish Congregations."

4. Personal correspondence with the author, March 20, 2015.

5. Rabbi Raskas alludes to his misgivings about the establishment of Beth Jacob in a 2005 United Fund and Council Oral History Project interview. "Interview with Rabbi Bernard Raskas." University of Minnesota Libraries, Nathan and Theresa Berman Upper Midwest Jewish Archives, January 2005. https://reflections.mndigital.org/catalog/jhs:983#/kaltura_audio.

6. The 1990 JESNA study of the agency had criticized what it characterized as an excessive emphasis on "values" rather than "academics" in the Day School. It was an odd criticism, given that it was, after all, the *Talmud Torah* Day School, the school was continuing to enjoy rising enrollments, and prestigious academic awards for Day School students were just around the corner.

7. In addition to the implementation of formal moral education curricula and the Inter-Communal Student Justice Committee Network, the Talmud Torah's moral education initiative led to repeated invitations to faculty to participate in local, regional, and national youth and adult synagogue education programs, Community Center educational series, education conferences, study groups, professional and organizational conferences (Jewish and general), summer camps, and school, synagogue, and community center staff in-service training.

8. *American Jewish World*, January 16, 1948, 8.

9. 1 Albert Gordon, in his *Jews in Transition*, a history of the Jews of Minneapolis, would emphasize George Gordon's role in fostering "unification" of the Minneapolis community, along with the role of the Talmud Torah of Minneapolis in the

founding of a community social service and recreation program, eventually leading to an independent community center. See Albert Gordon, *Jews in Transition* (Minneapolis: University of Minnesota Press, 1949), chapters 2, 9.

10. "A Portrait of Jewish Americans," 10–12. http://www.pewforum.org/2013/10/01/jewish-american-beliefs-attitudes-culture-survey/.

11. A sketch of a "Communal Curriculum for These Times" is offered in Appendix I.

12. "Generation Now: Understanding and Engaging Jewish Teens Today," 4–5. Accessed June 13, 2016, http://www.jewishedproject.org/sites/default/files/uploaded/PDF/Generation%20Now%E2%80%94Understanding%20and%20Engaging%20Jewish%20Teens%20Today%20April%202016%20Final%20for%20web.pdf.

13. Several such slogans are discussed in Earl Schwartz, "Tz'dakah, Tikkun Olam and the Educational Pitfalls of Loose Talk," *Conservative Judaism*, 63, no. 1 (Fall 2011): 3–24. Though potentially potent, overdependence on links of these sorts, including associations with camping, dependent as they are on the adolescent experiences of particular groups of Jews, can facilitate settings and practices becoming all too quickly dated and exclusive.

14. Interview with the author, June 11, 2015. Having lost its communal agency status, the "Talmud Torah of Minneapolis" now refers to a much-reduced grade 2–8 program managed by two Minneapolis Conservative Congregations. The Heilicher Minneapolis Jewish Day School has also seen a significant decline in enrollments.

15. See note 12 above.

16. Given these associations, a new name for the agency may be in order, though one that reflected the historical provenance of "*Talmud Torah*," the local agency's legacy, and renewed commitment to educational collaboration. "סנט פאול – ברית תלמוד תורה,/ *B'rit Talmud Torah.- St. Paul*/The Talmud Torah Covenant School of St. Paul" (the "B'rit Torah School" for short) would meet these criteria.

17. Gordon, "The Talmud Torah of St. Paul," 20.

18. Bernard Raskas, *Seasons of the Mind* (Minneapolis: Lerner, 2001), 76, 295.

19. E.g., Numbers 32:1–15, Deuteronomy 34, Isaiah 8:16ff, I Chronicles 22:29.

20. William Shakespeare, Sonnet 2.

21. *American Jewish World*, June 22, 1956, 14.

22. II Kings, 22.

Appendix I

A Communal Curriculum for These Times

When in the days of the second temple our ancestors sensed that the ground was giving way beneath the feet of the nation, they arose and compressed the national resources into "portable items" that would not be lost with the loss of the national homeland. The *religious faith*, the *literature*, and at the base of both, the *language*—this was the nation's "threefold cord" by which all the scattered parts of the nation would be connected and united through all of the generations to come.

—Ahad Ha'am, 1910 ("ריב לשונות")

In the preceding chapters steps toward reinvigoration of a communal base for Jewish education were explored. To reestablish such a base would pose formidable challenges, but even if such steps were followed, in St. Paul or other communities, is an educationally substantive, community-based curriculum still feasible?

In facing up to this challenge it must be acknowledged from the outset that effective Jewish curricula—educational plans that deeply engage both mind and heart—have never been the product of simple reversion to past formulas—though not simply because they are past. The need to "renew the old while sanctifying the new" has always informed the best of Jewish educational efforts. The extent to which curricula employed at the Talmud Torah of St. Paul have been successful *in* their time, can be attributed, in large measure, to being attuned *to* their times. They provided a comprehensible response to the perennial challenge: What for? Whether posed by the *hagadah*'s "*rasha*," or the "*hakham*," this challenge demands a meaningful response in, and for each generation. Jewish learning that both inspires and informs evidences such a response. In its first fifty years, the Talmud Torah's programs, while rooted in classical texts and traditional skills—curricula framed, to use Daniel J. Elazar's expressions, in "Hebraic national-cultural" terms—met with considerable success. Their particular synthesis of classical sources and contemporary experience proved a relatively good match for the tenor of the times. But continued educational success requires retuning to *these* times, and as best as can be envisioned, for the days to come. Jews have long understood that the Jewish life and learning is most fully realized, in Leo Baeck's words, at the juncture of "the day with eternity."[1]

One thing is certain. The caricature of the Talmud Torah of Minneapolis in Joel and Ethan Coen's 2009 film *A Serious Man* sets the standard for what Jewish education cannot afford to become. As in Philip Roth's "Conversion of the Jews" a generation earlier, the Jewish learning to which they were exposed (or subjected) in the 1960s is portrayed as flinching and faltering. The film was a parody, but to the extent it reflects very real, persistent impressions, it cannot be ignored. It's a bad sign when thoughtful adults look back on their Jewish education and remember only childishness.[2]

Leading the list of factors to consider in this regard, given preceding observations about the growing role of "voluntary choice" in Jewish life, is how to construct substantive curricula that parents will choose for their children, and as parents increasingly defer to their children when it comes to Jewish life choices, what youth will, themselves, find engaging.

As Daniel Libson and Ana Fuchs have argued, co-administration of multiple programs under the aegis of a single school or agency, as at the Talmud Torah of St. Paul, with room for parental choice among the programs offered, is a particularly effective and efficient way to provide educational alternatives that maximize programmatic accessibility and flexibility.[3] But choice, too, has its limits. As important as responsiveness to parental and student preferences may be, one would be hard put to name any type of education in which outcomes really matter—courses of study validated by the abilities and attitudes of those who receive it—that isn't built around a recognized core of skills and knowledge. Nevertheless, recent research on prevalent attitudes among Jewish youth, for example, the Jewish Education Project's *Generation Now Report*, suggests that a significant proportion of American Jewish teenagers do not view Jewish education in this way. This research has a great deal to tell us about where we stand, and can be helpful in crafting realistic educational starting points, but even the best description of what *is* cannot, in itself, determine *what ought to be*. Ultimately, charting a fruitful course for Jewish education begins at the intersection of inductive data and deductive goals.

CRAFTING A COMMUNAL CURRICULUM

A communal educational program requires a curricular framework that is, at once, rooted in sacred Jewish tradition, informed by the broad sweep of

Jewish historical experience, and responsive to the full range of human concerns and challenges. It must be attuned to diverse communal orientations and individual learning needs, and serve, potentially, as a foundation for curriculum development compatible with early childhood, supplementary, day school, secondary, and adult programs alike; a framework as far-reaching as Martin Buber's "Biblical Humanism," and as Jewishly articulated as Avraham Infeld's "five-legged table" metaphor for a strong and stable Jewish identity, constructed of "memory, family, covenant, Israel and Hebrew."[4] A communal core curriculum of this breadth and depth can be fashioned from the following elements:

1. *Hebrew language instruction. The particular blend of types of Hebrew (biblical, rabbinic, modern) may vary from program to program, but purposeful comprehension must remain a primary goal of instruction.*

   The Hebrew language weaves its way through each of the areas of the core curriculum. Historically, it has been the language most often shared by disparate Jewish communities. It remains the key to nuanced engagement with Jewish literatures, and is today the common language of the largest Jewish community, the Jews of Israel. "Hebrew is the nerve-center which unites and integrates the Jewish people in time and in space. It serves as an intellectual and emotional bond among all Jews throughout all generations, and throughout all the lands of dispersion. Its granite syllables are personal links to the timeless message of Moses or Isaiah. And by means of the Hebrew Bible and prayer book, Jews of the remotest corners of the earth are bound together." (William Chomsky)[5]

2. *Classical Jewish texts (beginning with Tanakh, Mishnah, G'mara and related midrashic sources), studied, whenever possible, in original forms and languages.*

   Jews hold in common, first of all, the words of the classical Jewish texts. Their implications and applications are often contested, but the sources themselves are shared, and continue to inspire and inform, despite these tensions. "Through this literature the reader can penetrate into the minds of people who devoted themselves to the seriousness of language and the sanctity of human experience. These texts represent a record of their struggles with the meaning of law, the nature of interpretation, the conflict of faith and reason and the elusive power of the divine. In reading them we come face to face with those issues that form the universal core of all great literature." (Barry W. Holtz)[6]

3. *A constructive recognition of Jewish diversity, historically and currently.*

   Jews have commonly described their past in dialectical terms—the priest and the prophet, *Beit Hillel* and *Beit Shammai*, Sadducees and Pharisees, Maimonides' supporters and detractors, *S'faradim* and *Ashkenazim, hasidim,* and *mitnagdim.* This tendency is, in fact, a simplification of a far more complex and diverse history. Thoughtful study of classical Jewish sources, and respectful engagement with varied contemporary forms of Jewish life, require an appreciation of this diversity, past and present, and its role in the development of Jewish social, cultural and political forms. The ongoing realization of the principle "*Haverim kol Yisrael*—All Jews belong" is a definitive characteristic of a communal approach to Jewish education.

4. *"Mitsvah" as a concept, and mitsvot in practice.*

   In the idea of "*mitzvah*" and the experience of being *mi-tsoovim*, all of the sub-categories of normative Jewish practice intersect. *Halakhah, din, hovah, ma'asim tovim*—all are rooted in, and derive their distinctive character from the *mitsvot* of Torah, both written and oral. While these derivative categories are often associated with cultural divergence, *mitzvah* as an overarching category remains Jewish common ground. Historically, intersecting obligations and responsibilities have formed the infrastructure of Jewish life. Jewish education as a glancing encounter with a menu of optional benefits isn't recognizably Jewish, or viable. "The force which undergirded the truths of Israel's life-view and translated them into daily routine—of home and marketplace, field and factory, school and sanctuary—was the dynamic folk conviction regarding Torah and *mitzvoth*. . . . The *mitzvah* was to be the diurnal, but existentially crucial, act of life prescribed in the divine teaching by means of which the universal 'ought' can be transformed for the individual, as member of the community, into a personal 'I must,' 'I can,' 'I will.' In a conjoined relationship, means and ends are fused into an indissoluble unity." (Norman E. Frimer)[7]

5. *Cultivation of the virtue of hoda'ah/hodayah (acknowledgment/gratitude) and its liturgical expression.*

   Acknowledgment of, and gratitude for the gift of all good things in life is fundamental to Jewish thought and practice, all contemporary Jewish movements, and all strains of Jewish liturgical tradition. Though the liturgical form of *br'akhah* is a reasonable starting point for learning about prayer, the *b'rakhah* is itself rooted in the more fundamental and eminently accessible practice of acknowledgement and gratitude, which is also a ubiquitous feature of Jewish liturgies. "Let us remember that it is not enough to impart *information*. We must strive to awaken *appreciation* as well." (Abraham Joshua Heschel)[8]

6. *The development of moral judgment and an ethic of universal moral regard; not simply the cultivation of attitude and habit, or the rehearsing of predictable platitudes, but the development of judgment.*

   The development of moral judgment, attuned to a universal regard for human welfare and dignity, along with the faith and fortitude that carries judgment into action, is inextricably bound up with the central premises of Jewish life. It constitutes a distinct field of learning, with implications that touch on all aspects of a Jewish curriculum. "You've been told, human, what 'good' means, and what God is asking of you: Only that you do justice, that you love faithfulness, and that you walk humbly with your God" (Micah 6:8).

7. *The Jewish week and year.*

The rhythms of Jewish time link Jews to one another, past and present, to the land of Israel, and to the eternal. As we tell time, we tell our story.

It is now often argued that if in the past such curricular elements, strongly influenced by cultural Zionist sources, provided tools for Jewish regeneration and engagement with the "larger world," they no longer do. In weighing this critique, it must be kept in mind that Jewish life and scholarship, even in the most ghettoized of circumstances, has been buoyed by the confidence that it is precisely *into* the real, "larger world" of mystery and wonder, moral integrity and social responsibility, that Jewish learning, rooted in these elements, leads. Nevertheless, the temptation to brush the "currently popular" with a thin Jewish patina and call it the "larger world" has long posed a challenge to Jewish educators. Students see through the glaze soon enough, and draw their own conclusions about what is real. A Jewish education that is more peel than pith also fails. A Prof. Hill "think method" of education might lead to a happy ending in the theater, but it's trouble in St. Paul, in Minneapolis—in any river city.

It must be acknowledged in this regard that adherence to a Zionist vision of regeneration has contracted in recent years, and may continue to do so in the years ahead. To the extent that Jewish life in Israel continues to inspire commitment to the educational elements presented above, curricula will be enriched by Israel-related components, but the synthesis must reflect current circumstances. Ultimately, these elements offer the most consistent, representative features of living Jewishly, and remain central to the educational programs of the congregation-based Jewish movements, irrespective of ideological and halakhic differences.[9] Together, they have proven a time-tempered framework for life-long learning and living "in the good graces of God and people alike," under an array of circumstances at least as daunting as those Jewish educators now face.

But these subjects do not teach themselves. Each requires skilled, informed, and devoted instructors, knowledgeable in content and pedagogical methods, and worthy of the requisite confidence of parents and students alike. Given these considerations, the prevalence of inadequate congregation-based educational programs, though communal cooperation might yield far more productive results, isn't surprising. All too often, such programs turn out, literally and figuratively, a penny wise and a dollar foolish, leaving

congregants ill-served *and* the community weakened. Regarding such unin-
tended consequences, the *G'mara*'s rule remains pertinent: *P'siq reshei v'la
yamut*?!/Detach the head and *not* expect it to die?[10] Communities, too, can be
severed in this way.

Ironically, congregational rabbis are in the best position to appreciate the
incompleteness—each according to its inadequacies—of their own programs;
best situated to appreciate that ideologically narrowed curricula controvert the
breadth and depth of the tradition, while time-starved programs inculcate the
lesson that Jewish life is itself haphazard and shallow. Regarding the second
of these points, a recent review of research on teenagers' involvement in Jewish activities actually indicated that contrary to the common call for reduced
contact hours to accommodate busy schedules, "the research demonstrates
that as involvement with after school activities increases among Jewish teens,
so does their willingness to participate with Jewish-focused activities," and
that "while some 'gateway' programming will likely be important, it will be
infinitely more impactful when it leads to sustained and on-going engagement." The same study also included in its "Key Findings" the observation
that "the current competition and fragmentation often observed [among
teen-oriented Jewish organizations] does not serve the needs of teens, nor
ultimately of the Jewish community."[11]

Communities that put off the challenges posed by such findings come to
resemble not so much the *hakham* or the *rasha* of the *hagadah*, but the *"eno
yode'a lish'ol*," who is no longer able to formulate the pertinent questions.
Thus, the crucial part local rabbis must play in articulating the contours of
excellent Jewish education and the institutional collaboration necessary to
provide it. This, however, will require a frank accounting, in this era of "life-
style enclaves,"[12] of what congregations are not accomplishing, due, to be
sure, to limited resources, low expectations, the modest expertise of instructors, and sectarian presumptions, but also because they are congregations,
not communities.[13] In recent years, for example, with the exception to some
degree of the local Chabad community, instruction in Hebrew to the point
of substantive comprehension of classical texts and contemporary Hebrew
has only been available for Jewish youth, in St. Paul, at the Talmud Torah.
Viewed from the perspective of a choices-driven culture, the Talmud Torah
alone provides parents and students the *choice* of substantive Hebrew language instruction in an egalitarian setting.

However, four caveats should be kept in mind in regard to curricular
reform along these lines:

1. Effective communal education not only calls for a collaborative institutional structure, and a willingness on the part of the community as
   a whole to support such a structure, politically and financially. It also

requires a manifest interest in the ensuing outcomes. The community must make clear that it values these outcomes at least as much as it currently lauds the very limited goals associated with the celebration of becoming a *bat* or *bar mitsvah*. On this point, liberal Jews have much to learn from their orthodox neighbors. In a world replete with compelling messages about the relative value of various forms of education, the Jewish community must make every effort to articulate its esteem for Jewish education. This appreciation must become an unmistakable feature of the communal ethos, substantiated in scholarships, work opportunities, and lifetime learning throughout the community. Jewish learners must know that their community eagerly awaits them, equipped with the learning they are acquiring. Robert Coles, writing about the broader challenge of "making schools better," emphasized:

> The issue is not only bricks and mortar, or even the techniques that our educational theorists urge upon us. The critical issue for many of our children (and for the rest of us, too) is purpose.
>
> . . . It involves giving both the adults and the children in a building a sense of hope, a faith that the daily rhythms in their classrooms really will amount to something important—helping to shape life itself and make it better as well. Tremendous energy becomes available to young and old alike when such a vision is accepted. It is that "secret," known to so many parents in their hearts, that a school can used to become transformed.[14]

2. Flourishing interest in educational uses of digital technologies should be viewed with due caution. There is, to be sure, much to be gained from the use of devices to meet specific students' needs for adaptations, in the teaching of Jewish history, and in language instruction. Curricula must not be left to settle back into methods and themes most familiar to the *instructors*, if more effective and fitting alternatives for their students are available. But the curricular landscape is strewn with erstwhile "exciting innovations," while the primary insight underlying the principle that Torah study is not complete without *Torah-sheh-b'al peh/* oral tradition is that a *true oral tradition necessitates face to face encounters between teachers and students*. The transference of much of oral tradition to written sources, accelerated with the advent of the printing press, while making *the words* more accessible, tended to obscure this definitive *personal* characteristic of oral Torah. Even among the People of the Book, medieval Jewish educators were familiar with the aphorism *meepee sof'rim, v'lo meepee s'farim*: "From scholars rather than from books."[15] Electronic media, through their increasingly effective mimicry of intimacy, augment this challenge significantly. The allure of novelty, efficiency, and economy associated with these technologies must not undermine

appreciation of immediate, person-with-person learning.[16] As Thoreau observed, when weighing the potential benefit of a new device or technique one can ill afford to ignore the pitfall of "too clever by half": "so with a hundred 'modern improvements;' there is an illusion about them; there is not always a positive advance. . . . Our inventions are wont to be pretty toys, which distract our attention from serious things. They are but improved means to an unimproved end. . . . As if the main object were to talk fast and not to talk sensibly."[17]

The best of educational intentions may be belied by methods that undermine the personal relationships and depth Jewish education demands. Embrace "amusement" as a standard of success rather than as one limited tool among many, to be used judiciously, and Jewish education loses twice: first in the resulting vacuity, and then as erstwhile Jewish attractions fade in comparison to main-street sources of diversion and entertainment students will inevitably encounter.[18]

3. Dashefsky and Lazerwitz's observations about a correlation between a growing proportion of American Jews who are "non-self-employed professionals" and lower rates of Jewish affiliation could be seen as incidental to questions about curriculum, or relevant, at most, in regard to related funding issues. However, this socioeconomic shift also has educational implications. The authors of *Habits of the Heart* maintained that the transformation of the American "professional" in the twentieth century from a figure firmly rooted in the moral life of a local community to an "open-ended," "success"-oriented occupational category has had far-reaching social and cultural implications. Commenting on this transformation, they observed:

> The profession as career was no longer oriented to any face-to-face community but to personal standards of excellence, operating in the context of a national occupational system. Rather than embedding one in a community, following a profession came to mean, quite literally, "to move *up* and away." The goal was no longer the fulfillment of a commonly understood form of life but the attainment of "success," and success depended for its very persuasive power on its indefiniteness, its open-endedness, the fact that whatever "success" one had obtained, one could always obtain more.[19]

These observations pertain to current circumstances in American Jewish communities as well. The prominent role of labor, manual and skilled, in the articulation of Jewish history and values becomes ever more problematic as growing numbers of Jews no longer see themselves in these identities.[20] Through the middle of the twentieth century, personal experience commonly resonated with *Pesah* motifs of unrequited Jewish labor, working-class solidarity (reinforced by neighborhoods), and liberation, but ever larger numbers of American Jews now find their legacy and socio-political purpose outside of their own Jewish communities, in the struggles of others for whom these experiences are far more immediate. Reaching out in this way can be ennobling, and bespeaks the deepest ethical duties incumbent upon all Jews, but it also suggests a growing inability of Jews to find themselves in their own story. In the past, Jewish communal identity was reinforced by the "affiliating" tendencies of its self employed and working-class members whose social position was, in turn, amply represented in classical Jewish sources. These affinities, which included both social and cultural bonds, are weakening. Jewish educators would be wise to take seriously the challenges posed by these changes.

4. Communal educators owe their communities meaningful and accurate, immediate and long-term evaluation of their work. Educational "success" means more than how many people come through the door. *Who* comes through the door, how long they stay, what they take with them when they go, what life-long influences can be discerned, and what impact the program has on the community as a whole are also important factors to consider in evaluating an educational program. Ultimately, evaluation must be on a generational scale: effective Jewish education is intergenerational, its content emphasizes processes that are trans-generational, and meaningful evaluation is multi-generational.

NOTES

1. For example, the *midrash* about a confounded Moses in Rabbi Akiva's classroom (B. M'nahot 29b). On reconciling "The day with eternity," see "Mystery and Commandment," in *Judaism and Christianity*, Leo Baeck, ed. (New York: Atheneum, 1970), 171–85.

2. Regarding previous efforts to outline central elements of a universal American Jewish curriculum, see, for example: Krasner, *The Benderly Boys*, 339–43. See also Leon Spotts, "Trends and Currents in Curriculum Development, 1930–1970," *Jewish Education*, 40, no. 4 (Spring 1970). On related developments in the Conservative movement, see Walter I. Ackerman, "Curriculum of the Conservative Congregational School," *Jewish Education*, 48, nos. 1 and 2.

3. On the continued advantages of joint day school—supplementary school programs, see Daniel Libenson and Ana Fuchs, "Day Schools, Disrupt! Why Day Schools Should Provide Supplemental Jewish Education." http://ravsak.org/day-schools-disrupt-why-day-schools-should-provide-supplemental-jewish-education.

4. See https://5leggedtable.com/. See also Barry Holtz's 2013 "White Paper," What Should Jews Know? (Is there a Core Curriculum? If so, What's Included?), http://blog.jtsa.edu/reframe/2013/04/04/what-should-jews-know/. Though Holtz works on the premise that "Benderly's vision of the communal Talmud Torah eventually gave way to the *congregational* school and despite some interesting experiments in recent

years, the overriding model . . . of supplementary school education is one based in an individual synagogue," his observations are nevertheless pertinent. See also Bill Robinson, "Striving for Shlemut: An Emerging Approach to Jewish Education," *eJewish Philanthropy*, December 19, 2018. https://ejewishphilanthropy.com/striving -for-shlemut-an-emerging-approach-to-jewish-education/.

5. William Chomsky, *Hebrew: The Eternal Language* (Philadelphia: JPS, 1957), 272.

6. Barry W. Holtz, ed., *Back to the Sources* (New York: Touchstone, 1992), 14.

7. Norman E. Frimer, "Law as Living Discipline: The Sabbath as Paradigm," in *Tradition and Contemporary Experience*, Alfred Jospe, ed. (New York: Schocken, 1970), 258.

8. Abraham Joshua Heschel, "The Meaning of Jewish Education," *Jewish Education*, 24, no. 2 (Fall 1953): 20.

9. In St. Paul, for example, from the Temple of Aaron website: "In preparation for a lifetime of active synagogue participation our students study a variety of view points and perspectives on important religious issues while always representing Conservative Judaism and its principles. The curriculum includes age appropriate instruction in Hebrew Prayer, *Tanach* (Hebrew Bible), other Jewish Texts, Israel, Holidays, God, and various other Judaic topics" (http://templeofaaron.org/education /schools/; Accessed October 25, 2016). From the Beth Jacob website: "We value children and adults as responsible partners in learning, together creating the next layers of our ongoing Jewish conversation. We value genuine listening that allows us to express and learn from multiple perspectives, creating a learning community in which each child and family is truly welcome. We value living in Jewish time and using Hebrew language; Jewish stories are at the center of our learning. We value a joyful, embodied, exploratory approach to learning, motivated by our children's questions and curiosity" (http://beth-jacob.org/education/youth-education/; Accessed October 25, 2016). From the Mt. Zion website: "We provide quality Jewish learning experiences for our students on topics including: ethics and values; God and spirituality; Hebrew; history and stories; holidays; Israel; Jewish arts and culture; life cycle events; rituals and celebrations; Shabbat; tefillah; Torah; tzedakah, and tzedek/ justice" (http://mzion.org/wp-content/uploads/2011/03/RS-Mission-12-12-12-Final -Draft.pdf; Accessed October 25, 2016). Not surprisingly, the Adath Israel website does not include an educational statement, as its members are mainly affiliated with the Chabad community, and for the most part, formal Chabad educational activities take place elsewhere.

10. *Shabbat*, 103a.

11. Michael Whitehead-Bust, *Current Trends in Jewish Teen Participation with Out-of-School Activities* (Denver: Rose Community Foundation, 2010), 6–7.

12. Bellah, *Habits of the Heart*, 71–75.

13. The chapter on "The Role of the Educator in Synagogue Transformation" in the anthology *Re-Envisioning the Synagogue* is indicative of this problem. Having noted the Kaplan-inspired "synagogue-center" model, the author observes that synagogues have continued to enlarge their "spheres of activity," and advocates developing intra-congregational collaboration to meet the ensuing challenges. The value of

community-wide collaboration, facilitated by educators, isn't explored. See Zachary I. Heller, ed., *Reinvisioning the Synagogue* (Hollis, NH: Hollis, 2005), 187–93.

14. Larry Martz, *Making Schools Better* (New York: Times Books, 1992), xii.

15. Simcha Assaf, *Meqorot le-Toledot ha-Chinnukh be-Yisrael*, Vol. 2 (Tel Aviv: Devir, 1931), 40, 49.

16. On the limits of the new technologies in Jewish educational settings, see E. Schwartz, "Oral Torah in an Electronic Age," *Conservative Judaism*, 49, no. 4 (Summer 1997): 32–41.

17. H. D. Thoreau, *Walden and Other Writings of Henry David Thoreau* (New York: Modern Library, 1950), 46–47.

18. On the ever-closer relationship between entertainment and religious life in the United States, see Neal Gabler, *Life: The Movie* (New York: Vintage, 2000).

19. Bellah, *Habits of the Heart*, 119–20.

20. For example, the high regard for manual labor in both Mishnah and Talmud; cf. Ber. 28a, Yoma 35b, Avot d'Rabi Natan 6, 49b, Ket. 105a, Yer. Baba Kama 10:10, etc.

Appendix II

Toward a St. Paul Communal Jewish High School Education Initiative

Brit *(covenant)*

We, the undersigned, are working to establish a new 8–12th grade Communal Jewish High School in St. Paul. The statements below have stood at the core of our work to this point. We now formally acknowledge them in this *brit* as we move into the next phase of our work to build a dynamic, strong educational institution that will open for all of our teens in September 2018.

We know there will continue to be challenges as we move forward, but share a commitment to our children's Jewish education, to the future of the St. Paul Jewish community, to *Am Yisrael* and to *Klal Yisrael*.

As we work toward a successful conclusion to this process, we commit to:

- Strengthen the Jewish community as a whole through this process,
- Strengthen the Jewish teen community of St. Paul,
- Create a high-level, dynamic, and engaging Jewish education for our teens,
- Offer a more robust program than any of the current High School programs can offer alone,
- Create an educational platform that is inclusive of all the needs of our youth and continues to meet future needs,
- Respect divergent understanding of Judaism and different ways of living a committed and authentic Jewish life,
- Give partners the benefit of the doubt, the space to listen, and to learn without judgment,
- Communicate and create opportunities for feedback with our stakeholders who are not around this table
- Honest, direct, and respectful communication with each other,

- Identify and recruit the volunteers and professionals necessary for the transition team and the task forces,
- Insure a communal financial commitment to the strategic planning and implementation of this institution, and
- Stay engaged throughout the entire process.

We sign this *brit* on behalf of ourselves and the institutions that we represent.[1]

NOTE

1. St. Paul Jewish Federation website. https://cdn.fedweb.org/fed-103/2/JFed%25 20Brit%2520covenant%2520letter5.pdf. Accessed January 27, 2019.

Bibliography

Adams, John, and Barbara Van Drasek. *Minneapolis–St. Paul: People, Place, and Public Life*. Minneapolis: University of Minnesota Press, 1993.

Alon, Gedalyahu. "The Lithuanian Yeshivas." In *The Jewish Expression*, edited by Judah Goldin, 452–68. New York: Bantam Books, 1970.

Amichai, Yehudah. *Patuah, Sagur, Patuah*. Jerusalem: Schocken, 1998.

Assaf, Simcha. *Meqorot le-Toledot ha-Chinnukh be-Yisrael*. Tel Aviv: Devir, 1931.

"Attorney General Humphrey visits Talmud Torah of St. Paul." *American Jewish World*, March 7, 1997.

Baeck, Leo. *Judaism and Chrisitanity*. New York: Atheneum, 1970.

Bellah, Robert, Richard Madsen, William Sullivan, Ann Swidler, and Steven Tipton. *Habits of the Heart*. New York: Perennial, 1985.

Bock, Geoffrey. *Does Jewish Education Matter?* New York: Council of Jewish Federations, 1975.

Boxer, M. "Revisiting The Non-Linear Impact of Schooling: A First Step toward a Necessary Corrective." In *Sociological Papers Formal and Informal Jewish Education: Lessons and Challenges in Israel and in the Diaspora*, Vol. 17. Sociological Institute for Community Studies, Bar-Ilan University, 2012–2013.

Brickner, Barnett. "Communal Responsibility of the Synagogue to the Jewish School." *Journal of Jewish Education*, Vol. 3, no. 3 (1931): 147.

Bryfman, D. *Generation Now*. New York: Jewish Education Project, 2016.

Buber, Martin. *Darko shel Mikra*. Jerusalem: Mossad Bialik, 1978.

Chiat, Marilyn, and Chester Proshan. *We Rolled Up Our Sleeves*. St. Paul, MN: United Jewish Fund and Council of St. Paul, 1985.

Chomsky, William. *Hebrew: The Eternal Language*. Philadelphia: JPS, 1957.

Cobin, Susan. Interview by the author, January 29, 2015.

Cohen, Steven, Ron Miller, Ira Sheskin, and Berna Torr. *Camp Works: The Long-Term Impact of Jewish Overnight Camp*. New York: Foundation for Jewish Camp, 2017.

Commission on Jewish Education in North America. *A Time to Act (עת לעשות).* Lanham, MD: University Press of America, 1990.

Connections Magazine. United Jewish Fund and Council of St. Paul (Fall 2011): 1.

Dashefsky, Arnold. "Does Jewish Schooling Matter?" *Contemporary Jewry*, Vol. 23, no. 1 (December 2002): 122, note 5.

Dashefsky, Arnold, and Bernard Lazerwitz. *Charitable Choices: Philanthropic Decisions of Donors in the American Jewish Community.* Lanham, MD: Lexington Books, 2009.

Dashefsky, Arnold, and Howard Shapiro. *Ethnic Identification among American Jews.* Lexington, MA: Lexington Books, 1974.

Dashefsky, Arnold, and Howard Shapiro. *The Jewish Community of St. Paul.* St. Paul, MN: United Jewish Fund and Council, 1971.

Elazar, Daniel. *Community and Polity.* Philadelphia: JPS, 1995.

Elazar, Daniel, ed. *Jewish Education and Jewish Statesmanship—Albert Elazar Memorial Book.* Jerusalem: Jerusalem Center for Public Affairs, 1996.

Elazar, Daniel. *The National Cultural Movement in Hebrew Education in the Mississippi Valley.* Jerusalem: Jerusalem Center for Public Affairs, Daniel Elazar On-Line Library, 1993. http://www.bjpa.org/Publications/details.cfm?Publication ID=2532.

Fine, David J., ed. *Responsa: 1980–1990.* New York: Rabbinical Assembly, 2005.

Finkelstein, Louis, ed. *The Jews: Their History, Culture, and Religion.* Philadelphia: JPS, 1949.

Gabler, Neal. *Life: The Movie.* New York: Vintage, 2000.

Gannes, A. P., G. Greenzweig, and George Pollack. *A Study of Jewish Education in St. Paul, Minnesota, 1977–1978.* New York: American Association for Jewish Education, 1978.

Gartner, Loyd P. *Jewish Education in the United States, A Documentary History.* New York: Teachers College, 1969.

Gavish, Ruth. Email correspondence with the author, March 20, 2015.

Geer, Lois. *1981 Population Study of the St. Paul Jewish Community.* St. Paul, MN: United Jewish Find and Council, 1981.

Ginsberg, Asher. *Al Parashat ha-Derakhim: Miv'har Ma'amarim M'vuar biy'dei Dr. Yermiyahu Frankel.* Tel Aviv: Devir, 1965.

Ginzberg, Louis. *Students Scholars and Saints.* Philadelphia: JPS, 1928.

Glatzer, Nahum N., ed. *Studies in Jewish Thought.* Philadelphia: JPS, 1974.

Glazer, Nathan. *American Judaism.* Chicago: University of Chicago Press, 1957.

Goldenberg, Kalman (Kokie). *United Jewish Fund and Council Oral History Project.* August 29, 1983. http://reflections.mndigital.org/cdm/compoundobject/collection/jhs/id/836/rec/152.

Goldring, E. B. "Building Community within and around Schools: Can Jewish Day Schools Measure Up?" In *Jewish Day Schools and Jewish Communities*, edited by A. Pomson and H. Deitcher, 33. Oxford: Littman, 2009.

Gordon, Albert. *Jews in Transition.* Minneapolis: University of Minnesota Press, 1949.

Gordon, Irwine. *Interview with Irwine Gordon*. United Jewish Fund and Council Oral History Project, October 10, 1982. http://reflections.mndigital.org/cdm/ref/collection/jhs/id/890.

Gordon, Joel. Interviewed by the author, February 16, 2015.

Gordon, Joel. "The Talmud Torah of St. Paul: A Picture of a Community School." *Pedagogic Reporter*, Vol. 34 (January 1988): 17–20.

Gordon, Louis. *Principal's Report*. Annual Meeting of the Jewish Education Center Association, May 24, 1932. Talmud Torah of St. Paul Archives.

Green, William D. *A Peculiar Imbalance*. St. Paul: Minnesota Historical Society, 2007.

Harshav, Benjamin. *Language in a Time of Revolution*. Berkeley: University of California Press, 1993.

Heller, Zachary I., ed. *Re-envisioning the Synagogue*. Hollis, NH: Hollis, 2005.

Himmelfarb, Harold. "Jewish Education for Naught: Educating the Culturally Deprived Jewish Child." *Analysis*, no. 51 (September 1975). Washington, DC: Institute for Jewish Policy Planning and Research of the Synagogue Council of America.

Hoffman, Marshall. "Temple of Aaron School Decision Riles St. Paul Jews." *American Jewish World*, January 14, 2000.

Holtz, Barry W., ed. *Back to the Sources*. New York: Touchstone, 1992.

Honor, Leo, and E. Picheny. *Social, Recreational, and Educational Survey of the Jewish Community of Duluth, 1944*. Minnesota Historical Society Archives.

Jewish Encyclopedia. Isadore Singer, Managing Editor. New York: Funk and Wagnalls, 1904.

Jewish Federation of Greater St. Paul Board of Directors Meeting Minutes, 2017–2018.

Jewish Federation of St. Paul Community Planning Process Findings Executive Summary, March 4, 2014.

Kahn, M. "Leadership in the Jewish Community." In *Tradition and Contemporary Experience*, edited by Alfred Jospe, 348–58. New York: Schocken, 1970.

Kaiser, L. I. "Minneapolis Is Different." *Jewish Education*, Vol. 50, no. 3 (Fall 1982): 34–38.

Katz, Morris C. "St. Paul Hebrew School Dispute." Letter to the Editor, *American Jewish World*, March 16, 1956.

Katz, Morris C. "What Are Really the Facts?" Letter to the Editor, *American Jewish World*, February 24, 1956.

Kaufman, David. *Shul with a Pool: The Synagogue Center in American History*. Waltham, MA: Brandeis University Press, 1999.

Kelman, Stuart, ed. *What We Know about Jewish Education*. Los Angeles: Torah Aura, 1992.

Klausner, Israel. *Vilna, Yerushalayim d'Lita*. B'nai B'rak: Beit Loh'mei ha-Geta'ot, 1983.

Kook, Abraham I. *Olat Ra'yah*. Jerusalem: Mossad ha-Rav Kook, 1983.

Krasner, Jonathan B. *The Benderly Boys and American Jewish Education*. Waltham, MA: Brandeis University Press, 2011.

Kroll, Janet F. "People of Vision See Dream Fulfilled at St. Paul T. T. Corner-Stone Laying." *American Jewish World*, June 22, 1956.

Kunz, V. B. *Saint Paul—The First 150 Years*. St. Paul, MN: The Saint Paul Foundation, 1991.

Leibowitz, Yeshayahu. *Emunah, Historiah, v'Arakhim*. Jerusalem: Academon, 2002.

Levine, Hillel. "To Share a Vision." *Response Magazine*, no. 6, 3–10.

Lipman, E. J., and Albert Vorspan, eds. *A Tale of Ten Cities*. New York: UAHC, 1962.

Lorenz-Meyer, E. A. *Gender, Ethnicity and Space: Jews in Minneapolis and St. Paul, 1900–1930*. Ann Arbor, MI: ProQuest/UMI, 2006.

Maimonides, Moses. *Mishneh Torah*.

Marcus, Jacob R., ed. *The Jew in the Medieval World*. New York: Atheneum, 1973.

Marcus, Jacob R. *United States Jewry, 1776–1985*, Vol. III, ch. 7. Detroit: Wayne State University Press, 1993.

Marsh, Kim. "Executive Director's Remarks." 50th Annual Meeting of the United Jewish Fund and Council of St. Paul, June 18, 1985. From the author's transcript of the talk.

Martz, Larry. *Making Schools Better*. New York: Times Books, 1992.

Mayer, Egon. *Parental Perspectives on Jewish Education in the United States*. New York: Center for Cultural Judaism, 2005.

McWilliams, Carey. "Minneapolis: The Curious Twin." *Common Ground*, Autumn 1946, 61–66.

Morphew, Clark. "Challenges for the Future." *St. Paul Pioneer Press*, April 5, 1996.

National Jewish Population Study. *Reports on the Study's Findings*. Council of Jewish Federations, 1975.

Newberger, Sara Lynn. Interviewed by the author, February 24, 2015.

Pertzik, Marvin. Interview with the author, June 25, 2015.

Pew Research Center. *A Portrait of Jewish Americans*. Washington, DC: Pew Research Center, 2013.

Pierce, Lorraine E. "The Jewish Settlement on St. Paul's Lower West Side." *American Jewish Archives*, Vol. 28, no. 2 (November 1976): 143–61.

Plaut, W. Gunter. "A Hebrew-Dakota Dictionary." *Publications of the American Jewish Historical Society*, Vol. 42, no. 4 (June 1953): 361–70.

Plaut, W. Gunter. *Mount Zion: 1856–1956*. St. Paul, MN: North Central Publishing, 1956.

Plaut, W. Gunter. *The Jews in Minnesota, the First Seventy-five Years*. New York: Jewish Historical Society, 1959.

Plaut, W. Gunter. *Unfinished Business*. Toronto: Lester & Orpen Dennys, 1981.

Pomson, Alex, and Howard Deitcher. *Jewish Day Schools, Jewish Communities*. Oxford: Littman, 2009.

Porter, Jack N., and Peter Dreier, eds. *Jewish Radicalism*. New York: Grove Press, 1973.

Portnoy, Eddy. *Bad Rabbi*. Palo Alto, CA: Stanford University Press, 2018.

Raskas, Bernard. *Interview with Rabbi Bernard Raskas*. St. Paul United Jewish Fund and Council Oral History Project. University of Minnesota Libraries, Nathan and

Theresa Berman Upper Midwest Jewish Archives, January 2005. https://reflections .mndigital.org/catalog/jhs:983#/kaltura_audio.

Raskas, Bernard. *Seasons of the Mind*. Minneapolis: Lerner, 2001.

Reich, Cindy. Interviewed by the author, March 17, 2015.

Rosenzweig, Franz. *Nahara'yim: Mivhar Kitavim*. Jerusalem: Mossad Bialik, 1977.

Ruffman, Louis L. *Survey of Jewish Education in Minneapolis*. New York: American Association for Jewish Education, 1957.

Sarna, Jonathan. *People Walk on Their Heads: Moses Weinberger's Jews and Judaism in New York*. New York: Holmes and Meier, 1982.

Schechter, Solomon. *Studies in Judaism*. Philadelphia: JPS, 1958.

Schick, M. *A Census of Jewish Day Schools 2013–2014*. New York: Avi Chai Foundation, 2014.

Schloff, Linda M. *And Prairie Dogs Weren't Kosher*. St. Paul: Minnesota Historical Society Press, 1996.

Schloff, Linda M., ed. "Who Knew? Stories Unearthed from the Archives." *Journal of the Jewish Historical Society of the Upper Midwest*, Vol. 6 (Fall 2011): 81.

Schloff, Linda M. YouTube interview, January 20, 2012. https://www.youtube.com/watch?v=m8Rn734i6Gs.

Schwartz, Earl. *Moral Education: A Practical Guide for Jewish Teachers*. Denver: Alternatives in Religious Education, 1983.

Schwartz, Earl. "Tz'dakah, Tikkun Olam and the Educational Pitfalls of Loose Talk." *Conservative Judaism*, Vol. 63, no. 1 (Fall 2011): 3–24.

Schwartz, Earl. "Why Some Ask Why." *Judaism: A Quarterly Journal of Jewish Life and Thought*, Vol. 53, nos. 3–4 (Summer–Fall 2004): 230–40.

Schwartz, Samuel. *Legacies from Jewett Place, and Other Memoirs*. Unfinished manuscript. Author's copy.

Seligman, Ben S., and Harvey Swados. *Jewish Populations Studies in the United States, 1948*. American Jewish Yearbook. Philadelphia: JPS, 1949.

Sheskin, Ira. *2004 Twin Cities Jewish Community Study*. Minneapolis–St. Paul: Minneapolis Jewish Federation, United Jewish Fund and Council of St. Paul, 2005.

Shluker, David, and S. Sterling Epstein. *JESNA Study of the Talmud Torah of St. Paul*. New York: JESNA, 1990.

Smith, Harold. Interviewed by the author, May 22, 2015.

Smith, Harold. *My Life: The First 95 Years*. St. Paul, MN: Celebrations of Life, 2014.

Spotts, Leon. "The Theory and Practice of Agency Mergers—with Special Reference to Jewish Education." *Journal of Jewish Communal Service*, Vol. 55, no. 3 (March 1979): 244–51.

St. Paul Community Planning Process Findings Executive Summary. Jewish Federation of Greater St. Paul, 2014.

"St. Paul Hebrew Schools Merge." *American Jewish World*, June 4, 1948, 18.

St. Paul Jewish Federation Community Planning Process, Priority 4: Strengthen Jewish Education. Final Report. St. Paul: Jewish Federation of Greater St. Paul, October 2018.

"St. Paul Orthodox Hebrew Institute Asks Public Support." *American Jewish World*, January 13, 1956, 1.

"St. Paul Unifies Jewish Education." *American Jewish World*, May 28, 1948, 1.

"Strategic Directions for Jewish Life: A Call to Action." *Jewish Philanthropy*, October 1, 2015. https://ejewishphilanthropy.com/strategic-directions-for-jewish-life-a-call-to-action/.

Teutch, David, ed. *Imagining the Jewish Future: Essays and Responses*. Albany: State University of New York Press, 1992.

Thoreau, Henry D. *Walden and Other Writings of Henry David Thoreau*. New York: Modern Library, 1950.

Tobin, G., and G. Berger. *Jewish Population Study of Greater St. Paul*. St. Paul, MN: United Jewish Fund and Council of Greater St. Paul, 1993.

Towards a St. Paul Communal Jewish High School Education Initiative: BRIT (COVENANT). https://cdn.fedweb.org/fed-103/2/JFed%2520Brit%2520covenant%2520letter5.pdf.

"Unified Education for St. Paul." *American Jewish World*, January 16, 1948, 8.

Vlodaver, Dalia. Interviewed by the author, May 5, 2015.

Walsh, James. "A Growing St. Paul Gets Hip to Millennials and Retirees Alike." *Minneapolis StarTribune*, May 24, 2015. http://www.startribune.com/a-growing-st-paul-gets-hip-to-millennials-and-retirees-alike/304828641/.

Wertheimer, Jack, ed. *Family Matters: Jewish Education in an Age of Choice*. Waltham, MA: Brandeis University Press, 2007.

Wertheimer, Jack, ed. *Jews in the Center: Conservative Synagogues and Their Members*. New Brunswick, NJ: Rutgers University Press, 2000.

Wingerd, Mary L. *Claiming the City: Politics, Faith, and the Power of Place in St. Paul*. Ithaca, NY: Cornell University Press, 2001.

Index

Page references for figures are italicized.

About the Author

Earl Schwartz is a member of the Hamline University religion faculty and former director of Hamline's social justice studies program. He is the author of *Moral Development: A Practical Guide for Jewish Teachers* and coauthor with Rabbi Barry Cytron of *When Life Is in the Balance: Life and Death Decisions in Light of the Jewish Tradition.* He has taught in a wide variety of community settings in the Twin Cities for more than forty years.